Going Home

Also by the Author

GOING
HOME

Tim Lilburn

ANANSI

This edition published in 2008 by
House of Anansi Press Inc.
110 Spadina Avenue, Suite 801
Toronto, ON, M5V 2K4
Tel. 416-363-4343
Fax 416-363-1017
www.anansi.ca

Distributed in Canada by
HarperCollins Canada Ltd.
1995 Markham Road
Scarborough, ON, M1B 5M8
Toll free tel. 1-800-387-0117

Distributed in the United States by
Publishers Group West
1700 Fourth Street
Berkeley, CA 94710
Toll free tel. 1-800-788-3123

House of Anansi Press is committed to protecting our natural environment.
As part of our efforts, this book is printed on paper that contains 100% post-consumer recycled fibres, is acid-free, and is processed chlorine-free.

12 11 10 09 08   1 2 3 4 5

Library and Archives Canada Cataloguing in Publication Data

Lilburn, Tim, 1950–
Going home / Tim Lilburn.

ISBN 978-0-88784-785-1

1. Ecology—Philosophy. 2. Environmental ethics. 3. North America—Environmental conditions. I. Title.

PS8573.I427Z468 2008   577   C2008-901068-X

Library of Congress Control Number: 2008922789

Cover design: Ingrid Paulson
Cover photograph: © Jonathan Kantor/Stone
Text design and typesetting: Ingrid Paulson

 Canada Council   Conseil des Arts
for the Arts   du Canada

 ONTARIO ARTS COUNCIL
CONSEIL DES ARTS DE L'ONTARIO

We acknowledge for their financial support of our publishing program the Canada Council for the Arts, the Ontario Arts Council, and the Government of Canada through the Book Publishing Industry Development Program (BPIDP).

Printed and bound in Canada

CONTENTS

INTRODUCTION

G EORGE Grant, in his monumental essay "In Defence of North America," that rumbling jeremiad beginning Technology and Empire, said descendants of European settlers never would be able to hold the gods of the New World as their own, so never would be "autochthonous" where they are, no matter how long the history of their stay on the continent might be. This rootlessness was ours, Grant explained, because of "what we are and what we did." What we are: detached long ago, while still in Europe, from that part of the Western intellectual tradition that would have taught us the suitability of "living undivided from one's earth," we cannot value what we most need, indeed cannot name it. What we did: we met the new land as conquerors and subjugated it. We moved too quickly over the ground, omnivorous, self-uprooting on principle, marked by the inevitably anarchic character of capitalism, to be shaped by where our bodies were. This homelessness of ours has proved disastrous both for human souls and for the colonized land.

Grant believed the ability to be fed by place was lost to North Americans of European descent because of our diminished capacity for the practice of attentiveness. Contemplation ceased to be ours when Reformation Europe severed its links to the thought of Greece and turned to a literally read Bible and to experimental science for sustenance.

. . .

Going Home attempts a resuscitation of a small part of this jettisoned tradition—the erotics of Plato, as they are found in his middle dialogues and his *Seventh Letter,* which are, as well, the erotics of Christian Platonists of late antiquity and the early Middle Ages. It is a book about conversation, a book about reading; it is a book of attempted retrieval; it is, above all, a long walk beside a line of texts — Plato's *Phaedrus* and *Symposium;* John Cassian's *Conferences; The Divine Names, The Ecclesiastical Hierarchy,* and *The Mystical Theology* of pseudo-Dionysius the Areopagite; and *The Cloud of Unknowing*—Europe's true erotic masterworks, in which a detailed account of desire, desire on the move, is set in place. It also includes a sporadic mulling of works on which the eight books under careful review depend— the *Odyssey;* Origen's *On First Principles;* Evagrius's *Praktikos* and *Chapters on Prayer;* the *Enneads* of Plotinus; Proclus's *Commentary on the Parmenides;* and Richard of St. Victor's *The Twelve Patriarchs* and *The Mystical Ark,* repositories of the West's deep, old stories, where an invaluable physics of the heart is stored.

Most of these books are no longer read. They, together with the few that seldom are, form a strand of thought so misrepresented as to be forgotten, a particular way of doing philosophy, a particular way of attending to the world. Eros plays a foundational role in the contemplative philosophy of Plato, who appears near the beginning of this tradition, as it does in the ascetical and mystical theologies of Christian students of Plato; indeed the contemplative life tracked throughout these works amounts to an account of the proper unfolding of desire, as it moves from idiosyncratic, pre-philosophical allegiances to the poverty and inventiveness of contemplative appetite. The incomplete description of desire flowering into contemplation in the dialogues is the substance of Platonic thought, precisely what he took philosophy itself to be. The long reading that follows perhaps will be an occasion of turning, of anagoge, of home-going, for those who take it in. A rejuvenated comprehension of longing, I believe, is the one way home for us.

. . .

I was born on the prairies but lived in many other places from my late twenties to early forties, mostly in Ontario and the United States, a Jesuit during much of that time, moving every few years from one apostolic assignment to another. I left the order in the late 1980s and worked on farms near Kitchener,

Ontario. When I returned to Saskatchewan a few years later, it was late summer. I had been lucky enough to land a job teaching philosophy and literature at a small Catholic college east of Saskatoon, but before I moved on to an acreage I'd bought with my then-partner in the area, I spent time in Regina, visiting family and rediscovering the city. I'd always had an affection for the Regina Public Library, a trim, modernist building across from Victoria Park downtown; with its tall windows and rows of books, it had been a refuge for me as I grew up. Late one hot afternoon, as I was leaving the library, a thunderstorm was threatening in the southeast, gigantic black clouds bulking over the Saskatchewan Power building. People were filing out of offices, getting into cars or catching buses; some Aboriginal men were gathered in the park.

I suddenly stopped on the steps, struck — immobilized — by the sense, the sure, sharp realization, that everything around me — the looming Power building, Victoria Park and its cenotaph, the beautiful First Baptist Church — were not *here* but seemed slightly dislodged and hovering, leaning elsewhere, their loyalties elsewhere, caught in a momentum of nostalgia for, obeisance to, distant centres of settler power, Winnipeg minimally, but more truly Toronto and the east, New York, London, the Europe to which the older buildings earnestly paid homage. The Aboriginal men, still moving and talking in the park, certainly were autochthonic; they rose effortlessly from the ground. But I did not, nor did the culture I came from, and I felt keenly this deprival.

It became clear to me, over the next several months, as Grant had sharply suspected, that my discomfort, which only grew, had every sign of being irredeemable. Dogmatic Christianity, Enlightenment reason, twentieth-century psychologies, the epistemologies, ways of being in the world most available to me, could not even recognize what troubled me, this feeling of floating where I was, and so had nothing corrective or consoling to say to me about it. Western philosophy, early modern and onward, does have much to say about ethics, which it traditionally sees as an achievement of reason and duty, but my concern lay beneath this with identity and with the possibility of a relationship with the land, a sort of larger body, where I found myself. I began to explore, with an energy greater than curiosity, the intellectual history that had formed me, probing for the vivid talk of that tradition's wisdom lineage. My anxiety to come home urged me to explore this tradition with little concern for conventional interpretations. It seemed impossible that I would find nothing there for someone in my predicament.

.   .   .

The close reading of Plato that begins *Going Home* indeed moves against the grain of almost all scholarship in ancient philosophy. The Plato who appears in these first two chapters is not the philosopher of systematic doctrines—the

Plato of philosophy departments—but of a contemplative practice arising from the correction, the training, of desire, for whom philosophy is therapeutic, the rescue of particular interlocutors from various jammed, contemplatively unfecund, erotic states. Such a reading of Plato while unusual is not novel; it draws light from such writers as Pierre Hadot and Zdravko Planinc; with less confidence, it listens to Leo Strauss in *The City and Man*. The readings of the Christian thinkers are equally heterodox, moving against a tendency in patristics to see most documents of the early Church as preoccupied by dogma. The Christian works scanned here are rooted in the same reading of Plato to be found in the earlier parts of the book, Plato the contemplative, Plato the ascetic, Plato the mystic; while not indifferent to doctrinal theology, they will be understood as primarily contributing to the Platonic maieutics of eros.

The exegesis of *Going Home*, it is hoped, also will speak both a philosophical and a literary poetics—a way of doing philosophy, a way of writing—and a politics. Contemplative philosophy or mystical theology, both accounts of the discipline of desire, provide the most trustworthy way of doing poetics, since poetry, like philosophy, like prayer, is more than technique: a poetics that is more than a study of craft is concerned with the life of desire and ascesis in which a particularly reaching sort of poem appears. The deep readings of Plato and early Christian students of Plato will reveal, as well, unexpectedly perhaps, a broad politics, an apokatastasis of all things, a pandemic return home, nonpartisan, nonanthropocentric, embracing human communities, yet reaching beyond their narrowly understood concerns: as Plato argues in the *Republic* (520a–d), the only authentic politics arises from extended contemplative practice.

. . .

Most critical accounts of Plato, many translations of his work, have the feel of having been written "on official paper," as Osip Mandelstam says of usual renderings of the *Divine Comedy*. The orthodox Plato is the Plato of towering, often inconsistent, theories on cosmology, the origin of the soul, epistemology, ethics and politics, an ontologically preoccupied thinker announcing "philosophical teachings"; it is not the Plato of the *Seventh Letter*, for whom philosophy is a "divine spark," (*Seventh Letter* 340) is an arduous practice of following desire within the context of a relationship with a guide. Read him from this second perspective and he realigns startlingly. The orthodox, theory-laden Plato offers no *logoi* on *poiesis*, is silent on the soul's return to nature; arch-rationalist, antipoetic, he seems simply to signal confusedly toward the Enlightenment. This version of Plato, coddled by a *jejeune* evolutionary theory of intellectual history, flatters the present, emboldens the present, but is not the Plato who makes an appearance in *Going Home*. The Plato stepping forward here will not be familiar in an awkward, foreshadowing way but strange in an oddly helpful way. The help he offers is psychagogic and touches on the erotic and the political.

Leo Strauss insists that Plato's works are not treatises but dialogues, and that "in none of his dialogues does Plato say anything." To lift some stand on knowledge theory, say, from the exchanges between Socrates and the geometer-educator Thedorous in the dialogue the *Theaetetus*, and suppose that this represents Plato's own view is equal to believing, as Strauss remarks, that Shakespeare himself held that life is a tale told by an idiot, signifying nothing. Nor will Strauss allow the argument that since Socrates widely is seen as the spokesman of Plato, what this figure says about cosmology or knowledge is Plato's own position, for Socrates is a master of irony, and to use such a master as a mouthpiece amounts to saying nothing: besides, Socrates himself insists that he has no teaching, that he has knowledge on only the matter of erotics (*Symposium* 177d–e, 212b; *Lysis* 204b–c; *Phaedrus* 257a–b). This is not a knowledge on which Socrates pronounces, but which he enacts, and enacts differently with each of his primary interlocutors in the middle dialogues. The point of these exchanges is not to communicate information, or to draw an individual to a particular point of view; they are therapies of desire that Socrates practises, with modest success, on more or less promising young men. Should this liberation be successful, these individuals will be fit for philosophy, the contemplation of beauty in its several forms. While Socrates's maieutics necessarily change with each conversational partner, each dialogue retains its capacity to act as a heuristic for any reader, that is, as a prod, a direction, to desire.

. . .

Origen's mode of reading—appearing in chapter three as a goad to John Cassian's ascesis of reading—is a "theological poiesis," that is, a discipline which is the making of a new life of deepened contemplative engagement.[1] All of Origen's thought, unsystematic, is merely a way of taking in writing that instigates and directs the spiralling of the attentive soul, an attention to imagery and story that grooves in interior change.

Poetics is usually thought of as the study of the mechanics within the making of poems. It inquires, thus, into the nature of metaphor, into prosody, stances to language and reference; but also, less usually, it is a look at the range of existential, spiritual, domestic, as well as literary, conditions within which poems grow—the poet's habitual reading, for example, where she lives, her family arrangements, who her friends are, whether she takes walks, where she takes them and for how long.[2]

Poetics, in *Going Home*, is alert to the interiority in which poetry flourishes; this poem-welcoming innerness, I believe, is the same as the interiority of one who practises philosophy, understood in the Socratic sense as an erotic, contemplative undertaking. It is a positionless permeability, an availability to daimonic things. A similar ascesis lies on either side of the poem: the reader, just as the writer before her, may be brought to such permeability; the poem growing from erotic practice is the one most likely to engender it. A philosophical poetics is the way that such an availability is fostered in an individual; it is the ascetical keeping of such a way. A similar preparation is crucial for poems "written on the front and on the back" (Exod. 32:15), poems that have an inner life, as well as a surface of music and image, and that can reach the inner life of a reader, works, that is, which permit an anagogic reading.

. . .

The politics within Origen's exegetical mystical theology, which are the completion of his therapeutics for the soul, are a healing, a return to nature, an apokatastasis, not just of the individual, but of the human world and the cosmos itself. Plato's mystical politics, much less eschatological, are more modest; the life of contemplation urged in the middle dialogues and elsewhere is more readily discovered and led in a city influenced by those who have completed the contemplative ascent and returned to the soul's first home (*Phaedrus* 247a–248b), and who now practise lives of unbroken attention. Contemplation is the sole source of virtue with both: for Plato, this virtue is foundational for the state; for Origen and other Christian thinkers of late antiquity, the various antinomies in being are erased as one rises in contemplation. While *Going Home* is not centrally concerned with politics but the unfolding of desire within the life of attention, it recognizes that this contemplation does have a political telos — *kallipolis* (the beautiful city), the Kingdom of Heaven — and that exegetical accounts of contemplative practice in Plato and

Christian Platonists necessarily touch on the disposition of contemplative courtesy that is the antipode of "that self-propelling will to technology," which George Grant said marked the versions of modernity of both the right and the left.

. . .

Going Home also delves into the epistemology of contemplation, the dependence of this form of knowing on discursive reason and on ontology, that reason's noblest fruit, together with contemplation's ultimate opposition to such reason and its accounts of being, indeed contemplative knowing's important task of undermining both. Chapter four, "Knowing as Ritual," looks at the cognitive training to which pseudo-Dionysius the Areopagite subjects his single interlocutor through the school of three books, *The Divine Names, The Ecclesiastical Hierarchy,* and *The Mystical Theology,* a linguistic ritual in which the subjectivity of the one who reads is painstakingly trued by, among other things, a recurring reprisal of cosmology, even as his attachment to the construction of cosmology is continuously weakened. Much of this training is liturgical, in which the presbyter to whom the three Dionysian works are addressed is formed by the observation, the enactment of ceremonial gesture, his learning not rational but theurgical, an alteration won by the penetrative power of numinal movements and objects—in particular the "statues" of apt words. Knowing here is entering ceremony's flow.

The author of *The Cloud of Unknowing*, a medieval disciple of pseudo-Dionysius, equally apophatic, is similarly suspicious of discursive reason in the furthest reaches of contemplation, wary of a dominant preoccupation with dogmatic theology in the interior life. Still, like the other contemplatives in *Going Home*, he is not a romantic vitalist, abandoning reason for some occult intuitive faculty; following Richard of St. Victor, he shows the initial role reason must play in contemplative practice, where, allied with the imagination, it both stirs and directs initial contemplative appetite. The erotic life, here as elsewhere in the tradition, is a healing of the life of reason, which is, in part, a shrinking of its sway. For *The Cloud* author, metaphysics, rather than being the end of theology, is an ascetical discipline breeding humility by placing the mind of one in training within the largest possible account of what is. As well as being interior training, this ascetical exercise of reason is political formation, fashioning deference in the contemplative before all things able to wake contemplative courtesy.

· · ·

Going Home will finish with a pair of personal chapters in which enactments of the contemplative practice under review in the larger part of the book are described. We are not from where we are, as George Grant observed; we, descendants of European settlers, do not come from this ground. We have the graves of ancestors here; we have spent a few generations scraping and shaving the land, but we have yet to take out chthonic North American citizenship. Some tasks are generational, and this one is so freshly started most of us are not even aware we have begun it, the work of making a home where we are. Perhaps, as Grant believed, this is an impossible task, but I am somewhat more optimistic.

Landscapes have exacting apprenticeships; these admit no shortcuts, such as the use of Aboriginal stories as if they were one's own paradigmatic accounts. European descendants in North America must find their own way of being where they are, something in their past that will show them a path to their idiosyncratic way of residence, a route back for them, a path home. There is, of course, much that seems catastrophic, place-erasing, in this past — an arrogant, anthropocentric Christian mapping of being, a Baconian, privateering union of experimental science, technology, and human enrichment. But it is from this past, some part of it, that we have to come: this, after all, is home as well.

I suspect that the way to where we are is through plain desire — and on this, on eros, its poverty, its leaping, the Western history of thought has much to say that is surprisingly acute. *Going Home* will speak again a few of the essential, virtually forgotten, works of Western erotics, beginning with the *Phaedrus*, in the hope that a probing, not-wholly-comprehending restatement can nudge a reader closer to what seems necessary but unenterable: the erotic life. This re-saying of books, these particular books, which are, in fact, silent parts of ourselves, strangely familial, will be a re-enactment of the flow of experience they sift and will bring perhaps a small interior correction. The fact that these books can be read in this way sets them apart from almost all modern ones. *Going Home* will be not so much exegesis, then, as apothegmata, remarks and lives sharing a single skin, initially, of Socrates, his interlocutors, and of Odysseus, the one he remembers and reimagines as model. We become what we attend to. Perhaps the books will be animals coming toward us out of the forest. So, as I've said, we will start to listen in on the talk with Plato's *Phaedrus*. But the ghost of Odysseus floats in this work, haunting, as it does in others.[3] So, first, Odysseus, with all his tricks, with all his turning, Odysseus, the sleepy one, the one who relentlessly sleeps.

I

One

PHILOSOPHICAL APOKATASTASIS:
ON WRITING AND RETURN

THAT one, the shining one: resourceful, rash Odysseus,
from whom no trick is hidden (*Iliad* XXIII. 730), the many-
minded man, the man of many turns, acrobatically witted,
that one, sleepy, skilful, much-contriving Odysseus, flight-
headed, who must stay seven years in a cave on a island "where
the navel of the sea is" (*Odyssey* I. 50); here he comes to weep for
home: none swears Menelaos, swears Antiklea, his mother
(XI. 216), has suffered like Odysseus; none has touched this
one's exemplary affliction. Calypso, his guard, celestial lover,
sole permanent inhabitant of omphalic Ogygia, Odysseus's
guide, is the daughter of Atlas, whose knowledge of the
underworld ("the depths of the whole sea") is pre-eminent,
Atlas who is the guardian of the tree-like way between heaven
and earth. His daughter promises to conceal nothing from
her weeping, unwilling lover, the versatile-minded wretch

insatiate in tales (XIII. 293): she shows him how to build the ship that will take him to within sight of the island of a people who are equal to the gods (VI. 244), through whom the gods ventriloquize their hidden minds (VI. 12), the Phaiakians who eventually will deliver the thought-bright man home. She gives him the adze and the double-bladed axe, occult tools, to build his ship; she takes him to the part of her island where alder, poplar, and fir inch to the heavens: by means of the heaven-entering trees he will make his way. Calypso is Odysseus's psychopomp, overseeing his purification, his instruction, bathing and clothing him in preparation for his journey, teaching him that he must accomplish all that he must do without "escort of gods." Other guides are the daimonic Phaiakians themselves, renowned as eros-like intermediaries: they offer the man of rapid thoughts their own thought-steered ships, "as swift as any wing or thought" (VII. 36), vehicles of ecstasy, as a means of going back, and lay him down in a levelling trance on the shores of Ithaka, exquisite goods from their perfect home stacked around him.

Odysseus's travels both before and after his incubation in the cave of Calypso—place of beauty and poverty, encircled with blooming vines, surrounded by fields of violet and wild parsley, the source of four rivers, a place where the birds sleep, near which Odysseus groans and pounds his heart with tears (V. 3), place of ravishment and compunction, a school of fundamental desire—his journeys to and from this hidden, infiltrating place are unlike ordinary voyages; like the hero Lemminkainen in the Finnish folk epic, *The Kalevala*—the "handsome man with the far-roving mind" (*The Kalevala*, 26. 31), the "reckless" one, the "rascal"—Odysseus's is an enchanted form of travel, filled with unrealism, including an underworld descent. He leaves Troy and sacks Ismarus, city of the Cicones, Thracian allies of the Trojans: up to this point his adventures, though heroic, are not outsized; but as he rounds Malea, carrying a goatskin bag of black, sweet wine, one part mixed with twenty parts water, given him by Maron, priest of Apollo, who lives in the tree-thick grove of Phoebus Apollo, he's driven off course (IX. 80–1) and suddenly what happens to him takes on the enormity of vision or nightmare. Giants, monsters, implausible acts—everything inflated, grotesque, the hyperbole of an unguarded psyche, shimmering with the exaggeration of ekstasis. Like the author-hero in the poem of Parmenides, like the seagoing servant hero in Skaay's Haida epic *The One They Hand Along*,[1] Odysseus travels spiritually now along the axis mundi, through an interior place of farouche exploit.

Odysseus's numinous adventures after rounding Malea have numerous shamanistic features, as has been frequently noted.[2] There is his ambivalent celestial marriage to Calypso, which, in part, launches his travels. There is the black wine of Maron, the "godly drink," known to few, resembling the trance-inducing mushrooms and tobacco juice Mircea Eliade says Ugrian and Jivaro ecstatics took. Maron lives in the grove of Apollo in northern Greece, home place of Hyperborean Apollo; this double association with the god points unmistakably to a daimonic calling. Aristeas of Proconnesus, a famous seer mentioned by Herodotus, a northerner as well, fell into a trance in which his soul was "seized" by Apollo: after this, he was capable of bilocation, his soul tumbling from him in the form of a raven as he accompanied the god. Abaris, also a northerner, also with powers to end pestilences and quell earthquakes, carried a golden arrow, standing for his link with Apollo and his capacity for ecstatic flight. Odysseus's seclusion in the cave on Ogygia, further, resembles the immurement of the traditional ecstatic candidate in the bush — Odysseus's "bush" is not only Calypso's cave but also the wilderness of the sea — during which his fellow villagers supposed him dead, devoured by monsters, by a god, so that when he returned he was not recognized but thought to be a ghost, just as Penelope supposes Odysseus dead and cannot see him as her husband when, at last, he speaks to her in their home. Odysseus's sleepiness, his "relentless sleep" (XII. 372) on several occasions throughout his journey, suggests the lethargic drowsiness typical of ecstatic candidacy, as well as the leaving of the body in trance; Chukchee shamans achieved their miraculous flight to the centre of the world, to the underworld, then into the celestial spheres, during such states in the "canoe" of the drum, their trance called a "sinking." The man of rapid thoughts, sleepy Odysseus, accomplishes his transit to Hades "in a black ship" (X. 503) and returns to Ithaka in thick slumber in a mind-driven craft. Odysseus's remarkable suffering, his god-fashioned disquiet, recalls the initiatory sickness or anxiety central to the shaping of ecstatics throughout northeast Asia.

The tree—poplar, birch, willow—appears repeatedly in the *Odyssey*; it is the same tree that in Siberian ceremonialism is the means by which one moves along the axis mundi, the cosmic tree itself, providing ingress to the world of the dead and the heavenly regions. Odysseus enters Hades, following Circe's instruction, through the poplar groves of Persephone, near which, a short way on, is the "moldy hall" of the underworld (x. 509–512); he arrives at the island of the god-equal Phaiakians in a craft worked from Calypso's heaven-touching grove; he saves himself from the pull of the Sirens, ensuring the continuation of his ecstatic journey, by having himself tied to the mast of his ship. The pattern and purpose of Odysseus's journey also has ecstatic qualities: a descent to the dead, ascent to heaven, effecting a restoration of political equilibrium, the original conditions of home. Like all mythic, interior travel, Odysseus's adventures involve the re-establishment of communication between earth and heaven—he eventually acquiesces to the gods—which in turn achieves the purging of social corruption. His ordeal, as with traditional ecstatic undertaking, effects a political as well as personal purification. But Odysseus is more than shamanic: he is the advance scout of something newer, the possessor of a cluster of qualities that Socrates in the *Phaedrus* will associate with the practice of philosophy. Indeed, Odysseus is a philosophical exemplar in his solitary apartness, in his large capacity for travel to extreme places both within himself and the numinal regions, in his burgeoning passivity to divine exigence, in his stripping, in his daimonic affliction, but above all in his affective apokatastatic nostalgia: the one thing he does not lose in the course of his unparalleled suffering is his longing for home. It is of just this form of single-heartedness that he is stripped.

.   .   .

First the *historia* of the *Phaedrus*, its ribald surface, then later its shimmering underlay of *theoria*, its recessed map of philosophy.

The book begins as Socrates meets Phaedrus, the youngish man for whom the dialogue is named, just as he, Phaedrus, is about to leave the city for a walk outside the walls, where he hopes, in country silence, to learn by heart a talk given earlier that day by the speechmaker Lysias, his much younger beloved, on the preferability of the nonlover as a sexual partner. Phaedrus has appeared before in Plato, in the *Symposium*, where he was called the father of the speeches, instigating the praises of eros with the complaint that too little reverence was shown the god (*Symposium* 177c). In his own encomium of desire in that dialogue, he showed himself to be a romantic sentimentalist: love is a great god, of immeasurable benefit to humankind, of especial benefit to beloved youths. Here we find him newly romantically linked with the sophist Lysias, a glittering, widely celebrated young author (*Phaedrus* 228a), and while Phaedrus remains credulous, we discover that he has shifted his loyalties from one idealism to another: it is the efficiency, the muscle, of charm in seduction that he now esteems.

He is completely bowled over by the virtuosity of the speech given by his beloved hours before—a copy of it bulges priapically beneath his tunic—its audacious trickery, purportedly usable by anyone, aimed at the importuning of a beautiful boy by someone who is not in love with him. The fact that the speech has nothing to do with any conviction on the part of the one who made it simply adds to its dazzle, makes it seem even more effortlessly masterful. Lysias has produced it as nothing more than a gleaming display of rhetorical ingenuity, a lit advertisement for his facility, yet Phaedrus is moved by the elegance and cleverness of these remarks as if they were actually beautiful (227c)—he responds to the glitter of Lysias's intelligence with Corybantic zeal (228b); as with love, the ersatz seems genuine to him. He greets Socrates with a shiver of delight (228b), seeing in him the perfect companion with whom to rehearse what he's heard this morning, since, he says, Lysias, "in a roundabout way," is interested in love, just as Socrates is known by all to be. Socrates agrees with Phaedrus's suggestion that he join him in his walk in the country and that he serve as an audience for Phaedrus's repetition of Lysias's speech; he repeatedly asks Phaedrus to lead him as they move away from the city; he seems helpless in his desire to hear what Phaedrus has heard; but as they begin their walk, it is Socrates who suggests that they "leave the path" and go along the Ilisus (229a). Phaedrus and Socrates are on a dialectical journey as soon as they go down to the river, an interior ranging, an Odyssean sailing.

The banks of the Ilisus, we soon see, are alive with psych-agogic import: a plane tree, sacred to Dionysus, god of wine and mystic ecstasy, stands near the water; from beneath it, the water appears to flow. The scene recalls Calypso's cave, that place of erotic instruction, school of sorrow and remembering, the grove in which it is set, the source of four rivers (*Od.* v. 57–73), but also numerous other depictions from the ancient world of the Tree of Life with the Water of Life flowing either beneath it or from it. The presence of the tree sacred to Dionysus, maker of a descent to the underworld to rescue his mother and an ascent to heaven, recalls the ecstatic labours of Odysseus.

Both Phaedrus and Socrates remark on the oddness of the place in Socrates's experience: he *never* travels outside the city walls; landscape and trees, Socrates himself declares, hold no interest for him (230c–d); he requires, it seems, Phaedrus's leading or that of another guide (230d) to move at all in this alien terrain. But, unexpectedly, it is the urban, humanistic Socrates who is most affected by the scene they have come upon, speaking with excitement on the beauty of the tree, the river, the grassy bank; Phaedrus is startled by his companion's strange effulgence. Later, it is Socrates who identifies correctly the mythical significance of the spot: it is near the place where Boreas, the god of the north wind, kidnapped Orithyia, daughter of Erechtheus, king of Athens. Socrates corrects Phaedrus, his supposed guide, faux psychopomp, who had assumed that the kidnapping had occurred precisely where they stood, not, as it did, two or three hundred yards downstream. Boreas lived in Thrace—Dionysus as well had associations with Thrace, the shamanic location—and had taken the king's daughter there, chthonic nature swallowing the city, where she gave birth to twin boys, both winged like birds. Boreas also is known to have lived in the shape of a horse and sired by the mares of Erichthonius twelve colts so soft of hoof that they did not bend the heads of the wheat as they galloped over a field or cause a ripple on the water if they moved on the sea. All Borean associations with the place suggest the power of ecstatic flight. An altar, Socrates tells Phaedrus, has been erected to the god of the wind, elemental force—in human form, he is always bearded, muscular—downstream where a walker would cross to pass into Agra (229c). Socrates later will speak of horses himself in religious ascent; horses, as well as ecstatic ships, as well as birds, were instrumental throughout the ceremonial religions of northern Asia, enabling ecstatic travel. Socrates, though out of place, is peculiarly intimate with the significance and beauty of the river, the tree, the slope: in such surroundings, with their suggestions of Dionysiac passion and transcendence, however, Lysias's speech, unmodified by the city, is reconfigured and its shabbiness, when Phaedrus gets around to reading it, shows clearly. In love matters, in matters of Dionysiac intensity, in the comprehending of the daimonic import of things in nature, the apparently bumbling Socrates proves to be surprisingly adept.

. . .

Yet Socrates, autochthonic, one who knows, declares himself to be unseated by Phaedrus's recitation of Lysias's speech: what puts him in ecstasy (234d), though, is not what Lysias says or how he says it but the effect of Lysias's words on his lover who is radiantly moved as he reads what his beloved has composed. Socrates is arrested by Phaedrus's permeability, the way the speech of another has placed a "Bacchic frenzy" in him; he is caught by Phaedrus's erotically intent passivity — this, after all, is his own philosophical stance, part of the "ten thousandfold poverty" his "devotion to the god" has brought him (*Apology* 23c). Phaedrus thinks Socrates is joking when he celebrates his delight; this is the second time Phaedrus doubts the seriousness of Socrates: the first time was when Socrates had been beside himself in praise of the Dionysiac scene they had entered, the bank slope, the river, the tree. Phaedrus does not think well about matters of emotional intensity: oddly, he does not recognize the category of things that includes the frenzy his beloved's speech has placed in him. Though he undergoes it, he does not note it or esteem it: it is not surprising, then, that he fails to cultivate it.

Socrates's own permeability, the substance of his philosophy, rests in part on his conviction of his ignorance — the one thing, aside from "erotic matters," about which he claims any knowledge (*Apology* 21d, *Phaedrus* 235c) — his emptiness, positionlessness; Socrates carries no speeches beneath his clothes. His insistence upon his ignorance here (235d), his insistence, a little later, on his incompetence (236d), is not ironic but is an assertion of his philosophical poetics: none of his ideas are his own; he assembles no system; he is "an empty jar," the words of others streaming through his ears (235d). But Socrates's reachability, his affective availability to the speech of others, is unlike Phaedrus's: it is modified by phronesis; through all that presses on him, he reaches for the one thing that corrects desire; he has not lost his wits as a lover (236a) as Phaedrus has; he has discernment. His self-awareness also means that he recognizes the frenzy his permeability places in him as a treasureable thing and he grooms it — later we will see how this grooming involves attachment to a particular form of memory.

His response to Lysias's remarks is lukewarm — the rhetorician, he says, just has "spoken in a clear and concise manner, with a precise turn of phrase" (234a), though, Socrates complains, he has repeated himself as if he had no real interest in his topic. The appraisal naturally staggers the enraptured Phaedrus. Socrates, with some clumsiness, goes further: he has no doubt that he can make not only a different speech — his breast is full, after all; he is not without interest (235c) — but a better one. He immediately regrets this boast, however, as Phaedrus presses him to give such a speech and sets conditions upon it — what Socrates says must contain more and better points without repeating any of Lysias's observations except the one that claims that the lover is mad while the nonlover is not. It is impossible, Socrates protests, for him not to appear a ridiculous dilettante before the shimmering professionalism of Lysias (236d). Phaedrus threatens to deprive Socrates of all reports of speeches in the future if he doesn't go ahead and make a competing speech, and Socrates, a "lover of speeches," feels his arm bent toward making some remarks of his own on the destructive madness of love, but he sets his own condition: he will cover his head as he speaks. Odysseus covered his head with his purple mantle in the court of Alkinoos out of shame for the tears he shed listening to Demodokos's account of events at Troy (*Od.* VIII. 84–6). The shame that Socrates feels during his initial speech, though, is less for his words than for their effect on the impressionable Phaedrus: he cannot bring himself to read their monstrous effect on his interlocutor's unguarded face. Unlike Socrates, Phaedrus is not aware of his permeability: he doesn't make his wits qualify it; he doesn't profess it, practise it, as Socrates does: in his sentimentality, he is the victim of his own availability.

. . .

Socrates's first speech, a head-covered speech, roughly traces Lysias's: Phaedrus cannot imagine any other sort of talk on love (235b); Socrates, true psychagoge, carefully does not exceed his anticipations. Since the purpose of Lysias's talk is the duping of a young man into granting sexual favours to an older man with no emotional ties to him, it works hard to undermine the position of the lover. The lover is contemptible, mad, ill, says Lysias; the lover is an amorous calculator, "keeping his eye on the balance sheet," giving the boy no more than a fair return for his acceding to sexual requests. The lover is naturally boastful—everyone will hear of his success with the boy—and he is untrustworthy in the long run as well: he inevitably will move on from his present beloved. His insecurity, further, makes him devious: he will starve the beloved of the friendships of the wealthy and intelligent, keeping him pathetically dependent. Everyone should feel sorry for the lovers, Lysias urges, not admire them as they usually do (233b). Nonlovers, on the other hand, are disinterested, magnanimous, generous, because they are not crazed, made possessive or irritably protective of their own dignity by love; they do not "follow us, knock on our doors," embarrassing the wanted youth with their ridiculous insistence. Love, says Lysias, is a disease so virulent that those who suffer it once lose all resistance to any new onslaught (231d). Even the lover himself is aware of himself as sick: he helplessly regards his inability to get himself under control; fully appreciating his chaotic state, he refuses to accept responsibility for decisions he made while in it.

Socrates pushes Lysias's strategic subversion of the lover over the top, writing the figure large as he does the "feverish city" in the *Republic* for his conversational partner there, Glaucon, that young man with slightly sinister political enthusiasms, who, like Phaedrus, has insufficient prudence to read the soul—and once more, the point of the distortion is to repel, nudging an interlocutor from a jammed erotic state. The lover, he says, has utterly lost his mind, is everything

Lysias says he is, deceitful, irritable, as well as being "absolutely devastating to the cultivation" of the beloved's soul (241c); imperious in his demands, he works out of a mad insecurity to make his boy weaker and inferior to himself (239a); the lover, older, is also physically disgusting, with parts that are "a misery even to hear...mentioned, let alone actually handle them..." (240d). But Socrates unexpectedly stops when Phaedrus assumes he is only halfway through: he has yet to praise the nonlover. He has, however, presented a lurid version of Lysias's lover — one so grotesquely drawn it must undermine even the tenability of the position of the nonlover — from which a supporter of the Lysianic position might be expected to recoil: he has given Phaedrus grounds to regret his enthusiasm. He halts because, he says, he has heard "a voice coming from this very spot," (242c) the numinal riverbank with its associations with chthonic gods, his daimonion, the divine voice that always turns him away from whatever "incorrect" thing he is about to do (*Apology* 31d, 40a). He says he sees now he has been impious in his denigration of love, which is actually, he now understands, "a god or something divine," (242e), and having said what he did is in immediate need of purification, the famous purification of Stesichorus, a palinode, a recantatory poem erasing what was said before.

Phaedrus misses much of this. He believes Socrates's speech to be an incomplete copy of Lysias's — he has conflated the two individuals from the beginning of the dialogue; he fails to see Socrates's remarks as caricature; he does not recoil from their exaggeration—and so for him Socrates's shame has a pedagogical significance: Socrates models for his interlocutor a way out of his infatuation with Lysias's glittering performance, his elegant simulacrum of insight, but Phaedrus is not reached by this piece of Socratic instruction: the nature of his permeability makes him ravishable but not educable.

· · ·

Socrates's reversal, his purification, is initially, oddly, a defence of madness. Certain forms of insanity, he says, are quite desirable, the words, we can imagine, rising in the intense listening of the erotic, the philosophical, individual. The beneficial insanities are mantic, engined by the god, driving one away from the lesser good of self-control (244d): they cause one to leave the path (229a); they drive one off course (*Od.* IX. 80–1), making those so afflicted out-of-place, disturbed (*Phaedrus* 249a), estranged in the Socratic manner (*Theaetetus* 149a); such a self-displaced, stirred craning, at its furthest reach, is the state of philosophy itself (249c–d), an alacrity, an erotic reachability not wholly unlike Phaedrus's delight, but pulled by an object that does not contort it to the disadvantage of an individual—a telos the pursuit of which unexpectedly unfolds the person into the musicality of virtue.

There is the madness of the oracle, says Socrates—the prophetess at Delphi, the priestesses at Dodona (244b)—who are "out of their minds when they perform that fine work of theirs for all of Greece"; there is the therapeutic madness, the sharp psychagogic, diagnostic inspiration, that discerns the individual in need of rites and purifications, lifting from them the guilt of ancient crimes (244d–e). There is the Bacchic frenzy the Muses place in particular poets, which drives their work past that of writers with mere technical mastery. A demonstration of such a superseding by one who has been driven out of his mind (245a) appears presently in the dialogue: Socrates, in the palinode, is Muse-goaded; Lysias is never anything more than clever.

Socrates then interrupts his taxonomy of benign, "god-sent" madness (245b) to give an account of what the soul is like, but admits that he can get no closer than an image to the actuality of the soul, since to say what the soul truly is would require, he claims, not only an exceedingly long account, but is a task only a god could manage (246a). Yet he makes an attempt: the soul, he says, is like the union of a charioteer and a team of horses, both of which are winged, like the mind of Odysseus, like the offspring of Boreas and Orithyia: one of the horses is beautiful and good, while the other "has the opposite sort of bloodline" (246b). The wings of the soul—all of the soul is winged—are what is most divine about it and, thus, divine things—wisdom, beauty, goodness—cause them to strengthen; foul, ugly things atrophy them (246e).

The winged human soul, at some early point, joins the procession of gods, led by Zeus, heaven's commander, whom the other eleven deities follow: the procession moves through heaven "looking after everything" (246e), each god accomplishing a particular cosmological task: anyone who wishes to follow them may—there is no jealousy among those who are divine. They begin their ascent to the banquet at the rim of heaven, and the god's chariots move easily to that place—they have exquisite balance, after all, are compactly under control—but human souls who follow them have difficulty, the bad horse, heavier, unruly, pulling the chariot back to earth. What is visible from the rim of heaven is beyond description, yet it speaks directly, nourishingly, to intelligence, offering it intuitively certain, nonreportable views of justice, interior order, knowledge—contemplative clarities "of what really is what it is" (247e).

The soul that "follows the god most closely, making itself most like the god" (248a), gets at best only a partial view of the colourless, shapeless, intellectible things beyond heaven's rim; the head of the charioteer, struggling with his horses, rises a little "up to the place outside" and sees what lies beyond for a moment, then is pushed aside and down again as other chariots fight to the rim (248a–b): if its partial view of what is true is insufficient, it loses its wings entirely and falls back to earth. The soul's wings may be regrown, but this involves the lucky, relentless work of a number of lifetimes and requires that a soul consecutively chose, through a series of rebirths, the life of a philosopher, or, what is virtually the same but somewhat less unlikely, the life of a lover of beauty or a person tending to erotic love (248d).

A philosopher's mind grows wings because in memory it keeps close to what it has seen; like Odysseus, the philosopher does not fail to recall the quintessential nourishment of his original state. One does this by maintaining an alert receptivity to those reminders of the unparalleled, extracelestial things, such as the beauty of a young man. Eccentricities flourish in this remembering; people think the person so recollected is "disturbed and rebuke him for this"; the divine possession is invisible to all (249d). Such recollections cause one to be cast out of one's life, mantically alacritous: one, then, is caught up in the fourth, the paramount, the sublating, madness, which is philosophy: the pre-eminent moment in this frenzy, this particular ekstasis, is the appearance, through memory, of apokatastatic desire.

· · ·

Odysseus achieves his passage to heaven-like Phaiakia by way of trees cut from Calypso's grove, assembled into a boat under her instruction; the Altaic shaman enters the celestial home of Bai Ulgän carried by the soul of a light-coloured horse that has been sacrificed in front of his specially erected yurt, its spine broken after a birch branch has been passed over its back, no blood being allowed to touch the ground or the sacrificer during this ceremony. The traveller in the Socratic palinode moves to a point beyond the rim of heaven in a chariot pulled by one good horse and one bad horse, physical forms, it is usually thought, for the contesting powers of reason and the passions. For all three, the ascent is accomplished with sexual emotion—Odysseus desires a return to Penelope; the philosopher's ascent begins when an apokatastatic nostalgia is quickened in him by the repeated sight of a beautiful young man; the ecstatic travel of a Siberian shaman is powered by his erotic love for his *ayami* or tutelary spirit.[3] The palinode has no ontological significance: it sets in place no dogmas about the nature of the soul or its life before birth; it makes no theological claims; it has nothing to say about the physical structure of the universe. The Socratic account of winged ascent is nothing more than a heavily wrought, action-filled image meant to render the soul (246a) for an interlocutor, Phaedrus, who loves speeches but has demonstrated an incompetence in the reading of souls. It is also a heuristic intended to lure and shape desire, which evokes nothing other than the full range of desire's secret, almost unspeakable imagination, which the desirer, if he experiences it at all, experiences strangely as nostalgia: full erotic reach appears as remembering. The beauty of the boy is not the only source of anamnesis: a heuristic tale like the ascent account in the palinode works just as well. Phaedrus repeatedly sees resemblances of the surpassing things—he is quite attracted to such things, speeches, beautiful, young males—but he does not remember because his senses do not discern adequately what is before them (249e): he cannot see moral beauty, of course, justice, moderation, but also he cannot fully fathom physical beauty or literary resonance. Neither takes him anywhere; neither quickens in him the eros that is philosophy.

. . .

So Phaedrus and Socrates sit on the riverbank in the heat of the afternoon, talking, talking. The day is hot; the stream is cool.

Beauty is one of the radiant things the soul saw as its head momentarily lifted above the high rim before it was yanked downward by the team it could never control, that had never stopped pulling, before it was shouldered aside by other enthusiastic souls keen to see "that blessed and spectacular vision" in the hectic, noisy moment of rapturous insight: feathers broke off in the melee and forgetting immediately began. Other things were visible in this roiling moment—justice as it is, wisdom as it is—but they receded further with the soul's descent into the body, so that now the only way to "follow the god's pattern" (253b) and return to what feeds the soul is through erotic love. The only way to do philosophy is through erotic love, philosophy as an interior availability to something that seems to be nostalgia and from which gathers a desire to re-experience the purity of what appears to be ultimate vision—thus the philosophical need of the bad horse: all of the soul is winged (251b). Philosophy can be done only under these conditions because vision, says Socrates, is the least decayed of the senses; beauty, as a result, is the only one of the ultimate things that still comes through to human beings. When it is manifest to a "recent initiate" in the form of a beautiful boy, the person is flattened by an erotic wind, pain and joy; what he feels is the residue of his recent heavenly ravishing; it is a longing for the past (250d), which he construes as a love for an individual. The soul, with some trauma, returns to its feathered state. One becomes mantically single-minded—propriety is forgotten, one's friends, family, one's affairs are forgotten—thinned to one wanting. But pursuit is not all: the lover is impelled to secure an initiation for the beloved: his love madness must be transferred to the beloved and such a transferral is impossible if the beloved is not romantically captured (253c). Philosophy, certainly, is the erotic reach for the young man, but it is also the young man's reception of the lover's maieutical goodwill; this communicates into him what the lover knows: displacement from his life, a sort of affliction, a leaving the path, which marks the beginning of a long apprenticeship in emulating the god (253b).

.   .   .

In the discussion of rhetoric that takes up the last third of the dialogue, the old issue of the difference between Phaedrusean and Socratic permeability is revisited. Phaedrus, a good Lysianic, rests lightly on his loyalties: his admiration for Socrates's palinode nudges him to turn on his beloved, reporting a recent conversation with a politician in which Lysias was attacked as a mere "speech writer" (257c). Socrates objects to the condemnation: it's not writing itself that is shameful—one *could* write well, he claims—but speaking or writing shamefully or badly (258d). But then what distinguishes good writing from bad, he wonders. This question goes to the heart of Phaedrus's character; he is enamoured of books, of writers—all writers are good, all books impressive. He admires Lysias's lack of roots, lack of place; his being a writer brings him this: the cleverness of Phaedrus's beloved means he never locates himself in a view, the writteness of his speech means that what it says is portable, usable by anyone under almost any set of circumstances. Because he isn't embodied, nothing limits Lysias's audacity—his shocking charm, his noble wilfulness—making him, in his caprice, appear *atopos* and god-like.

Socrates warns Phaedrus that as they try to answer the question of quality in writing, they must be careful to pass by the Siren-like influence of the cicadas who overhear them. The cicadas, sounding in the trees throughout the hot afternoon above the two speakers on the riverbank, were once human beings themselves, Socrates says, who when they first heard the Muses sing were overwhelmed by the pleasure of the experience, forgetting to eat and drink in their rapt delight; they died in this state without even realizing they had done so (259b).

Part of their role now is to report to the Muses human beings who are devoted to the arts and give to these persons "the gift from the gods they are able to give" (259b), that is, they can make those they report dearer to the Muses by making their devotion known. The cicadas themselves are not particularly dear to the divine singers—they are granted the doubtful gift of being able to indulge their monomaniac listening without interruption for eating and drinking—

nor are they devoted: they perform no art. A being seduced by a thing is not an honouring it: such immolation is a form of wilful self-absorption, not devotion, not honouring. The virtuosity of the cicadas is merely vocal; they don't actually say anything; they are Lysianic; not only are they not dear to the Muses, they do not profoundly hear them; not hearing, they are not spoken through. Because they have been seduced, they can't bring a listener to any depth; they can charm, but they can't bring one to divine places. They have greed but no madness. Phaedrus is cicada-like; he immolates himself before authorship and the fetishized artifact of the book, disappearing in his own ravishment; he is caught by the romance of the book and the romantic placelessness of the author: he carries a book under his cloak next to his skin. The charm of authorship not only immobilizes him; it keeps him on the surface of writing. He esteems the mere power of being able to move someone, to exploit a basic permeability in a listener, the muscle of the sophist, seeing this as the height of achievement and not simply the "preliminary" of philosophical maieutics (269b–c) — such is the primitivism of Phaedrus's own erotic availability.

Socrates, on the other hand, is dear to the Muses: he serves Calliope, muse of epic poetry, by doing philosophy (259d), that is by replicating in his acts, his erotic craning, the ecstatic heroism recounted throughout epic literature from Sumerian poems of Inanna's descent, through the *Odyssey*, to the unnamed servant's passage to the land beneath the ocean in Skaay's *The One They Hand Along*. The one difference between

the psychagogery of Socratic rhetoric and ecstatic travel is
that, though both involve the direction of souls in the underworld, Socratic direction is never funereal: it draw souls, as
in the Cave allegory recounted in the *Republic*, into some
unsayable light.

. . .

Good speaking and writing, Socrates argues, comes from
one who knows the truth of his subject (260e); it is devoted
to "directing souls...not only in the law courts but also in
private" (261a). Bad writing, then, simply ravishes those
whose permeability is without discernment; it enchants but
takes one nowhere: instead it immobilizes the soul, robbing
a person of eros and its motility, its epektatic appetite,
Agathon's performance, Glaucon's blueprint for the imperial
city, working the erotic deformities of charm's fat sleep and
dogmatism. Knowledge of the truth of one's subject comes
through the dialectical practice of collection and division,
where all things of the same kind—all forms of madness, say,
all forms of love—are drawn together (265e), then separated
into species, cut along "natural joints," the "left-handed" sort
of madness being discarded, the right-handed valued (226a–b).
Not all can do this: only those who have undergone the anamnetic experience either through a self-quelling desire for a
beautiful youth or through a speech inspiring apokatastatic
nostalgia would be able to perform this diaeresis, this slicing:
anyone unengined by such memory could be no more than

self-ministering, holding in a partisan manner to whatever view of "justice" or "love" most pleased him, no play in his erotic life, conviction misconstrued consistently as understanding.

Good speech also requires a study of the nature of the soul, its various types, and the effect different speeches are likely to have on various sorts of souls; such knowledge comes by means of "a long rough path" (272c) that no one would attempt unless he had an ambition "to be able to speak and act in a way that pleases the gods as much as possible" (273e). The ability to read souls taxonomically cannot come from written accounts of rhetoric, which systematize address, shrinking the complexity of maieutics to a manual; this perpetrates the deception that lies in all writing—that the reproduction of an experience is equal to the undergoing of the experience; it does not confess the vicarious nature of writing itself. Codified, written instruction on rhetoric, like all writing that takes itself with a fatal seriousness to embody knowledge of lasting importance (277d), confuses representation, here analysis, with the thing itself (275c), imagines it identifies without remainder. Socrates has in mind works on the mechanics of rhetoric by the peers of Lysias, purporting to teach the skill of arguing what is likely—an endeavour that, even with goodwill, he believes to be fraudulent. It distances one from what one would know—it breeds forgetting (275a): apokatastatic remembering is an erotic enterprise and grows, at least in part, from an experience of poverty. The conditions for this poverty are erased in the identification of system with understanding: writing that takes itself as unparalleled achievement truncates desire. Apodictic, exhaustive, it gives the impression that it yields clear and certain results (277d), analysis confused with authority: yet it is only the simulacrum of the term of inquiry. In fact, such writing is not even inquiry since it is no longer appetitive, epektatic. If system is taken as anything other than training or heuristic, if it is held to be a terminal state, it de-eroticizes inquiry. Phaedrus cannot imagine any inquiry beyond system and its application as technique.

. . .

Odysseus arrives home because it has not left his imagination since his heart was broken during his seven years sequestering in Calypso's cave: an Odyssean stripping is the mother of erotic imagination. The lover of the youth loses himself—all sense of self-protection, all dignity—and the memory of home strides toward him: out of humiliation, a building attention; out of an initiatory affliction, an apokatastatic reaching. A systematic analysis of the soul that does not efface itself breeds a bogus sufficiency, inattention. But writing from someone with "a knowledge of the truth," who can defend his writing when challenged, who can make an argument that his writing is of little worth (278cd), reminds one of one's original nature, of what one has always known but never said to oneself. Such writing can contribute to the philosophical enterprise, the quickening of an affective apokatastatic nostalgia for an event that never occurred, the report of which draws in the whole of desire, its full stride, its unabridged imagination, and starts one on the way home. The *Odyssey* and the Socratic palinode have the power to entice into being the erotic endeavour they represent—a vivifying, frightening undertaking, which will go on beyond the poem and the tale of chariots wrestling into the sky.

Two

WHERE DESIRE GOES

SOCRATES had two teachers when he was young, the physical philosopher Anaxagoras and a woman from Mantinaea, the mysterious city of prophecy, Diotima. He also reports that he spent two periods as an autodidact, one before his encounter with Anaxagoras's thought and the other following it, when he tried to work Anaxagorean mechanisms into a complete teleological explanation of the universe. At the end of his education, he claimed to know a single thing—the "erotic matters" taught him by Diotima, the daimonic woman, queller of plagues: these, he insisted, made up the whole of his mature philosophy (*Symposium* 177d–e, 212b; *Lysis* 204b–c; *Phaedrus* 257). But Socrates's knowledge of erotics is peculiar: potential lovers complain of his unerotic nature; Socrates himself insists on his own sterility (*Theaetetus* 149b): he brings nothing out of his own. This knowledge that he claimed to possess, moreover, is astonishingly slight, just as his powers of divination are (*Phaedrus* 242), just as is his capacity to distinguish among beautiful persons (*Charmides* 154c): he presents it at one place as the meagre ability to distinguish lover and beloved at a glance (*Lysis* 204c). What is it exactly that Socrates, with strange imperfection, with such modest reach, knows? And how does this make a philosophy? The singularity of his oddly qualified knowledge of desire also seems to demand an explanation. Is the fact that Socrates knows *only* erotics haplessness, or a peculiar coincidence — or is something meant by the solitariness of this knowing?

His earliest intellectual efforts were spent trying to find a complete explanation of physical reality, a line of inquiry directed by "the general question of the cause of coming into being and perishing" (*Phaedo* 96a). He says he experienced "a remarkable enthusiasm for the kind of wisdom known as natural science" in this search, thinking it "magnificent to know the causes of everything" (96a). He was first drawn by an account of cosmogenesis, which theorized that life grew from primordial slime, itself the putrefactory result of a meeting of cold and hot substances, a view associated with Archelaus. He later worked through a number of hypotheses concerning the origin of thought — that it came from the blood, from air, that it came from fire; later still, he considered the possibility that reason grew from the brain's ability to manage hearing, sight, smell, these forming the basis of memory, the beginning of knowledge. He said that he went "backwards and forwards" on these ontological and epistemological questions, finding no clarity, until he came to a moment of epistemological crisis, where struck with "such complete blindness," he seemed to be unlearning what he previously knew. He became convinced then that he had no gift for the sort of physical inquiry that had driven him and decided to give it up immediately.

He happened to overhear someone reading aloud from a fragment of Anaxagoras in the street a short time later, however, and was delighted to discover in what he believed he heard a cause, Mind, which "arranges all things in order and causes all things" (97c). His interest in physical philosophy returned with force. But, in fact, he had misheard Anaxagoras's position. Socrates wanted Anaxagoras to give him the fullest possible account of physical reality—teachings on the roundness of the earth, the geocentricity or nongeocentricity of the universe, the velocities and orbits of the stars—and also to show him how these features were best (97d–98a). A closer investigation revealed to him that Anaxagoras was not interested in design but in efficient causality and he was thrown down again "from a marvelous height of hope" (98b). He entered yet another crisis in thought, more extreme this time. He had believed that Anaxagoras would have revealed a universal final cause, the good that bound all things together and made each individual in the most providential way. In his disappointment in finding such a cause—the presence and source of benevolent design—by examining physical reality, he entered a second period of self-directed thinking, in the course of which he came upon "a second best method" by which he decided to work from hypotheses rather than observation. This is the method of *dianoia*, of discursive reason, sketched in the figure of the divided line in the *Republic (Republic* 511a). He saw this new method as failure even before he seriously set out on it, though, a looking at things in their images that he fell into because he was afraid of complete blindness of mind if he looked at them directly with his eyes (*Phaedo* 99d). Hypotheses are rather weightless, simply the propositions that one judges to be soundest and thus honours. His subsequent examination of hypotheses themselves eventually led him to the ultimate teleological account of being he sought — but this discovery hinged on a later knowledge of the beautiful.

Socrates came to be troubled at the end of his enthrallment with the natural sciences by the reductive tendency in physical accounts — such and such is beautiful because it "has a bright colour, or a certain shape or something of that kind" (100d): attachment to such explanations made the emotional shadow of an encounter with beauty — the jolt, the humbling of such an encounter — vanish; it plucked eros from inquiry, made inquiry a form of greed. There seemed to be no communication between the two *logoi*: attachment to one foreclosed on the other: the older, erotic Socrates thus "can no longer understand or recognize those other learned causes" of which the physical theorists speak (100c). Little of his previous training in physical philosophy — except this disappointment about the explanatory limits of physical accounts — seems to have been transferable to what the mantic woman wished to teach him. With her, he proved to be a remarkably unpromising student, passive, speechless, inappropriately swept away, inspiring scant confidence in his teacher. She seemed a poor pedagogue as well: she repeatedly discouraged her pupil from wonder; she questioned his ability; she kept her instruction incomplete.

With Diotima's teaching, Socrates was forced to recognize that his education could not be an unbroken progress; in fact, his earlier interests acted as a block to receiving her new teaching: they could not be added to what she revealed about erotics. He himself later came to see the construction of complete systems as items of knowledge as a false start in philosophy, naive, merely scholarly, laughably detached (*Theaetetus* 174a–b). The place of science is within the erotic life about which the pure Thalean speculator knows nothing.

Socrates's pre-Diotimean impulse was to acquire knowledge: she sought to substitute an inclination to be ravished by beauty, thus she discouraged his ambition to comprehend and urged on him an erotically alert passivity. She tried to nurse him from his noetic activism; this deprival would leave him vulnerable to the blow of beauty.[1] He would be drawn by beauty, would be disappointed by it; he would be unmanned, dislodged from self-consciousness, rendered centreless in the pull exerted by beautiful things — and he would come to see this erotic wrestling as knowledge. He would no longer reach for circumscription, apodictic naming, because something beautiful manifest as beauty — rather than as an item of knowledge whose beauty is discountable — is experienced as out of reach, and one is inevitably epektatic, on the way, with regard to it. Thus, the encounter with beauty breeds humility; what one wants is always distant, unlike. The individual will be momentumed by this not having, made erotic. A training, then, an ascesis, takes place within the attraction to beauty, a quickening of virtue: one's pleonexia, concupiscence, the amassing of sufficiency is muted. A deluded sense of interior prosperity, that particular stasis, home-owing, is altered into a fleet poverty.

. . .

When Socrates returned from the army following the defeat at Potidaea, as Plato tells this story in the *Charmides*, he immediately visited the palaestra of Taureas to meet old friends and learn the current state of philosophy in Athens. Who, he wanted to know, stood out among the young in wisdom or beauty or both? Charmides, he was told, towered above the rest, chiefly because of his astonishing good looks; these were matched, moreover, his cousin Critias assured Socrates, by preternatural intellectual achievement: the boy already was a philosopher and a strong poet (*Charmides* 155a); Critias himself had assisted him to these heights. Socrates expressed a keen desire to speak with the boy; his subsequent meeting with Charmides provides an instance of the operation of beauty.

Charmides's appearance is as the others said: it creates amazement and confusion in all around him (154c), including Socrates, who is tongue-tied when the beautiful boy sits beside him on a bench in the gymnasium. His confidence that he might be able to handle this exchange leaves him immediately; he is awkward (155c), bent back, inept before the marvellous youth. Then, as Charmides leans toward him to ask a question, Socrates happens to catch a glimpse inside of his tunic—the garment of one who is absolutely perfect in his nakedness—and he is upended by the buck of desire. Astonishment, appetite, abashment—hallmarks of an encounter with beauty. Socrates stumbles through the first few moments of his conversation with Charmides, over-whelmed by the lion-like aspect of the beloved (155e) yet flung forward by an insistent eros. Beauty speeds and thins: it breeds a disarming single-mindedness.

Socrates sees before long, though, that Charmides's charm is somewhat other than it appeared at first: Critias has claimed that his cousin was flawless in both mind and body, his temperance (*sophrosyne*) equalling his remarkable appear-ance. It is as if his beauty were of such magnitude that it seems obvious that it would be total, spiritual as well as phys-ical, but something appears to be missing. Charmides may not have allowed his good looks to turn his head—he aspires to an orderly "quietness" in behaviour—but he shows no real knowledge of the virtue he is said to possess. Either Critias's lack of understanding concerning wisdom (his con-fusion of this matter becomes clear as the dialogue progresses) or the false confidence Charmides's beauty provokes has inspired his misidentification as someone wise. As Socrates's conversation with him continues, the boy himself comes to realize that he has not even the knowledge he previously believed he possessed: he ends by confessing his complete ignorance of the nature of any virtue attributed to him (176a). Entering a period of noetic freefall himself, he per- haps becomes teachable. The dialogue ends shortly after. Socrates, in this exchange, has correctly distinguished the lover from the beloved, as he said he could, and has drawn circumstances toward the truth he has discerned. The beloved becomes the lover at the end of the dialogue, Charmides pronouncing himself keen to be engaged daily by Socrates. There may be a beauty that does not erase one's poverty, something that remains distant, always the beloved, that allows one to remain erotic before it, but it is not, it seems, what Charmides has to offer.

. . .

The narrative arrangement of the *Symposium*, Plato's central dialogue on desire, is comically convoluted. Apollodorus tells the story of Agathon's party, and the speeches there praising eros, to an unnamed interlocutor by reporting an earlier account delivered to someone called Glaucon, who has heard a garbled, misleading version from yet another, who has received it from a man named Phoenix. He (Phoenix) had heard it, but mixed up what he heard, from Aristodemus, a disciple of Socrates, who had also told large fragments of the story to Appollodorus, a current follower of Socrates. Appollo- dorus has checked some of the details of Aristodemus's ragged story with Socrates himself; satisfied with its rough truthfulness, he says he will tell it in the very words Aristodemus used. The party, about which surprisingly much curiosity still remains, occurred "a very long time ago"; at its most dramatic point, the conversation contains an account of an even older exchange between the young Socrates and his mysterious teacher of erotics. One gathers from all this complexity that philosophy by nature is removed from the everyday; the distance in time of the reported conversations underscores this as well: philosophy is difficult to access; a maze stands before its entrance; philosophy is a hidden thing. Further, these conversations on desire are reported as taking place at night within an enclosed garden: philosophy is hidden. Still, it frailly lives, in a partial form, in a series of imperfectly recalled conversations that are handed down, yet even in this state, it continues to exercise an oddly attractive power.

The dialogue is an account of a drinking party at the home of the writer Agathon; present are Agathon's friends and his lover, Pausanias. Each attending the party agrees to give a speech on love in lieu of heavy drinking; they have been deep into wine the night before and still feel the effects. Socrates arrives later and is the last to speak: his speech is not original but a report of remarks made years ago by his one real teacher, Diotima, the daimonic woman, his rough-handed guide. The dialogue concludes with the loud, drunken appearance of the ferocious and lovely Alcibiades, a one-time unsuccessful seducer of Socrates.

Socrates appears at the beginning of Aristodemus's story uncharacteristically shod and bathed; he's gone to unusual lengths to prepare himself for this social encounter, but not, apparently, out of honour for his host, Agathon, who has just won a major literary competition. Socrates, we quickly discover, did not take the trouble to attend Agathon's elaborate victory celebration the previous day, an event that amounted to a public anointing. Trepidation, we soon learn, stands behind Socrates's fussing with his appearance: he begs a reluctant Aristodemus, whom he eventually sends on alone, to accompany him to Agathon's dinner, drawing a comparison between their going and Diomedes and Odysseus's infiltration of the Trojan camp in Book x of the *Iliad* (*Symposium* 174d).[2] Hector just has laid a dispiriting defeat on the Greeks, and, as the night advances, a sleepless Agamemnon finds his courage fading as he stares out at "the innumerable fires burning in front of Ilium," as he listens to "the music of the flutes and the reed pipes, and the voices of the troops" (*Iliad* 10. 10). So, it seems, does Agathon's raucous celebrity appear to Socrates. The enmity of the other guests to Socrates, however, is not immediately clear; he is welcomed, and when Eryximachus suggests that their drinking accompany encomiums to eros, Socrates readily agrees: what they wish to praise is the one thing he knows with any facility. But what Socrates says stands apart from the speeches of the others: all other symposiasts, we see, treat eros as reified, other, as a god, a force of nature, an exigence in the psyche dispassionately observed — none attempt phenomenology to speak of eros, but turn to theology, physics, or psychology. All do ontology in some form; none confess the whipping presence of eros in themselves. None of the other symposiasts, indeed, are erotic, none impoverished, in pursuit of what is beyond having; all angle for some overlook of knowledge, some easy advantage, sexual, professional; Socrates alone has taken on the identity of eros itself. Eros, among those who praise it yet are unerotic, is in an enemy camp. There the daimon also is bumptious. Socrates has none of the fluency of the other speakers in their praise speeches: he can do little more than report what eros has done to him as he's been caught up in this momentum and altered by its dumbfounding.

· · ·

Agathon, the host of the dinner at which desire is praised, has won a competition for poetry with a tragic poem that astounded thirty thousand Athenians; he has hosted a large victory party from which he still has a hangover. He now hosts yet another celebration for a select group of friends — a Dionysiac par excellence, it appears, an adept at nearly all the god's undertakings: deep drinking, sweeping poetry, public, triumphant ecstasy. Socrates, a renowned drinker himself and thus perhaps a favourite of the god, has snubbed Agathon at his previous celebration, and Agathon now is on tenterhooks to see if Socrates will play the same trick again, this time before Agathon's closest friends and his lover: he sends for Socrates shortly after Aristodemus's unexpected arrival, but Socrates, who has fallen behind his friend and is now standing in a neighbour's doorway absorbed in some contemplation, has sent the boy back. As the dinner begins, Agathon repeatedly orders his servant to go again and demand that Socrates follow him to the courtyard, but each time Aristodemus dissuades him. This is just his way, Aristodemus soothes the increasingly wary and anxious host. The combat between Socrates and Agathon—Ais and Hector, Diomedes and Hector—has already begun.

Socrates finally arrives, interrupting the dinner at mid-point, momentarily usurping Agathon as the centre of attention; the latter attempts to remedy this by inviting Socrates to lie beside him at the far end of the table, thereby drawing the eyes of all once more. He digs at Socrates just as the other is settling in, saying he wishes him near so that by touching him something of the wisdom that occurred to Socrates in the doorway will be transferred to him like wine moving along a twist of wool. Socrates expresses doubt that touch communicates insight, remarking further, tellingly, on the flash, youthfulness, and conspicuousness of Agathon's own wisdom (175e). Agathon notes the insult, and promises that he and Socrates will "go to court" about their respective wisdoms in time, with Dionysus himself appearing as judge. This is in fact what happens unexpectedly at the end of the dialogue, with Socrates emerging as the clear Dionysiac victor: he drinks both Agathon and Aristophanes into oblivion as he instructs them on a unitary version of the tragic and comic arts about which both are ignorant (223d).

But Agathon's non-Dionysiac nature is clear well before
the end of the dialogue: he confesses to Eryximachus even
before the speeches begin that he lacks the strength for heavy
drinking (176c). Agathon is not a genuine initiate of Dionysus,
and one must wonder therefore just what he can know of
eros, for as Alcibiades later insists, erotic madness is identi-
cal with Dionysiac madness (215d–c). The other symposiasts
also must fall under suspicion: they find much to praise in
Agathon's exquiste encomium to eros and none object when
Eryximachus makes him Socrates's equal in desire (193e).
All agree, moreover, to drink little. Agathon has not truly
entered the mysteries of Dionysus, nor of Eros, though his
glittering reputation claims otherwise. Socrates, on the other
hand, is indisputably Dionysiac, as Alcibiades later makes
clear in comparing him to sileni and satyrs, both known to
be followers of Dionysus, just as he, we soon see, is an authentic initiate into the mysteries of eros (212b).

Socrates enters the enemy camp when he appears in
Agathon's courtyard, though only he is fully aware of this.
And he enters in a brilliant, comic, insolent disguise, ready
for philosophical combat: he comes in the form of his host's
attractiveness; bathed, shod in "fancy slippers," he wears as
camouflage the ersatz accessorial "beauty" that is all Agathon
can muster. Socrates looks slightly ridiculous decked out so:
he mocks the man he visits by going to lengths to replicate
his host's thin beauty in a body far from beautiful. Even in
his writing, Agathon aims only for the shimmer of physical
beauty, mistaking this for depth. And in this Agathon has

been Hector; in this, he's inflicted a wound on Socrates, on eros since Socrates is eros, on philosophy since eros is philosophy. He disarmed thirty thousand Greeks two days earlier, winning them over to the supremacy of mere attractive speech by simply entertaining them; being so entranced has been offered as a substitute for the interior life poetry might quicken. He's de-eroticized them, those whom he regards as fools (194b).

. . .

The matter of drink absorbs much time at the beginning of the dialogue — the question of how to drink, various disinclinations to drink, Agathon's lack of strength in drinking, the health risks of drunkenness — there are signs everywhere that Dionysus is being eased out as a presence in the coming discussion of eros, so that the desire addressed here will be relieved of madness.

Eros without Dionysus is useful like salt (Phaedrus); is a ready apologia for the seeking of self-augmenting sexual gratification (Pausanias); is a force of nature, a corporealized divine providence understood as a principle of science (Eryximachus). But in all this, it is not eros that the symposiasts praise; what the others talk about are mechanisms leading to one's self-enhancement: there is not a whisper of self-transcendence in all of the pre-Socratic positions. None, aside from Socrates, are erotic, none reaching, though all are full of theory about desire. Agathon's own encomium is only decorative, melodious. Socrates offers it faint praise; all the others acclaim it. Socrates's own remarks provoke little comment, aside from a complaint from Aristophanes that they suspiciously resemble his own. There is no understanding here. Aside from the unreliable Aristodemus, who seems to be paying only partial attention and who eventually nods off, the one truly erotic man is alone until nearly the end of the dialogue.

. . .

Socrates announces that what he will say about eros will not be beautiful, suggesting that beautiful speech, distinguished by fluency and comprehensiveness, speech taking a pleasing shape determined by its author, marks a misunderstanding of eros. His words will be halting, gathered without pattern, falling "as they come" (198e). Socrates, though he places himself among "those who do know" (198e), is not fully articulate on the matter of eros; he cannot give an architectonic account; he cannot begin his speech in full possession of the *logoi* of what he describes; and in this, his talk mimics the range of eros itself, which knows in a manner between wisdom and understanding, yet uncannily hitting correctly on what is (202a), though unable to offer a full account of it, unable to speak systematically on the nature of reality and how one knows it. All the individual who knows erotic matters can do is report what he underwent; to be in possession of a theory of desire, of beauty, of goodness, is to betray one's uninitiated

state. Those who are erotic, like Eros itself, then, both know
and do not know; like Aristophanic lovers who remain with
one another through life, yet cannot say what they seek from
the other (192c), who would accept in a moment fusion with
the other—this would mean a return to their ancient, unitary, circular nature—but who can say little of this, the soul
divining what it wants dimly and speaking it in riddles
(192c–d), the erotic individual is both expressive and dumb.

Socrates's halting, ragged, awkward speech, placed largely
in the mouth of another, is one way of saying roughly what
the god is (199c); his demeanour, however, is a more eloquent
revealing of eros. His inarticulacy is eros's, as is his lit, yet
darkened, understanding. Socrates's estrangement at
Agathon's gathering is also a rendering of the daimon. He
has set himself out of place, arriving late, refusing to give the
same sort of eulogy as the others; this is of a piece with his
general eccentricity, illustrated by the incident of his standing in a nearby doorway, contemplatively alert, abstracted,
refusing repeated requests to come to dinner. Socrates is neither of, nor not of, the party. Eros, as well, is neither within
nor without, neither god nor mortal, yet, as daimon, in communication with both (202e). Eros, further, as Diotima's
ascent account underscores, throws persons out of place; to
be erotic is to be ecstatic; eros perpetually renders one homeless. Socrates bears this mark of eros: he is *atopos*; he is
"always dwelling in neediness" (203d), never unaware of his
incompleteness, his marginality from what he most elementally seeks perpetual. He communicates placelessness to

others as well, drawing them from fixed views, as in Charmides's case, or from entrenched ways of life, as he does with Alcibiades. Estranged, finally, he is an intermediary, like the daimon, standing here between what the mantic woman teaches and those enchanted by mere beautiful speeches. One report of eros is the contortion a person undergoes in becoming erotic.

· · ·

Eros is a physician (186c); eros is a skilled hunter who "plots to trap the beautiful and the good" (203d). Eros is a magician, druggist, sophist (203d), and a diviner. Eros is a philosopher, necessarily because it "is love in regard to the beautiful" (204b); it philosophizes through all its life, the reaching inevitably endless (203d); it is a philosopher, moreover, who cannot give an account of what he knows (204b).

The multiplicity of Eros's identifications has the variety of unbridled praise; it also has the appearance of apophatic speech where names are subverted — the residue of the affirmation retained, however, in the negation — in an effort to nudge language toward a rendering of ineffability. It also resembles — like the noesis of hitting correctly on things, the single type of knowing of which eros is capable — the knowing which is a true sort of pointing.

Eros is a philosopher, and so lies between being wise and being without understanding; its philosophizing reaches no term; it cannot say what it does since it has no overview of its activity, yet it is not without an aim. Nothing in the dialogue, however, accounts for eros's intentionality, except for the weak assertion that it serves and attends beauty—which it also relentlessly hunts—because it was conceived on the day of Aphrodite's birth. Such hunting is a healing, a divining, a conjuring, a balm, a knowing.

Eros also is Socrates, later in his life, shoeless, homeless, far from beautiful, always poor, but, Poros-like, alacritous, "always weaving devices," epektatic, courageous, inventive, keen for practical wisdom, never without a scheme to trap the object of his headlong pursuit.

· · ·

Socrates, for all his soon-to-be-uncovered erotic nature, is remarkably passive throughout his reported exchange with his teacher, Diotima, the perhaps invented, or augmented by invention, queller of plagues. The young Socrates twice places himself unequivocally, helplessly, in her hands (206b, 207c), declaring an unbudgeable ignorance on erotics: he can see no headway possible outside of her teaching. During the latter part of Diotima's account of the lesser mysteries of desire and throughout the whole of her "perfect revelations" about eros, Socrates is completely speechless, as if he's effaced himself entirely from the conversation. He may be a pliant student, but he is not a promising one: when Diotima asks him why animals "are all ill and of an erotic disposition" when it comes to procreation and the care of their young,

and he confesses he can think of no reply, she asks him dispar-
agingly whether he really thinks he will ever become skilled
in eros at all (207c). She doubts his ability on other occasions
as well, most pointedly when she questions whether he has
any hope whatsoever of being initiated into the higher dis-
closures of desire. She chastises him for his amazement at
three points in her instruction (205b, 207c, 208b), the first
time when she speaks of the universality of eros and the latter two times when she touches on the sexual and domestic
activities of animals. His amazement is a kind of helplessness
before what appears to be extravagance in her teachings; it
amounts to a refusal to go as far as she leads, a general preference for what he has always known.

Socrates had a theory of eros before meeting Diotima
even while something has led him to seek her out. He believed
that Eros was a great god, that he was beautiful, and lived in
human beings as a love of beautiful things (201e); that while
everyone desires, only a few love, while the great many do
not (205b); that loving, the desire of good things, is not
endemic to human nature. Indeed, his earlier views have the
romantic elitism of such beautiful souls as Pausanias and his
lover Agathon. Diotima's persistant interest in animal sexual
intercourse no doubt would sit ill with the fineness of
Socrates's early erotic beliefs; she goads him in this; troubled
and uncomprehending about this unusual preoccupation of
hers, he can say little. Diotima does not supply Socrates with
another position on eros so much as she impoverishes him
in what he previously held. In the revelation of the lower

mysteries of desire, it is not that he is being instructed but that he is being emptied. Thus he becomes more like eros itself in the course of their initial conversations: he is made homeless from his positions; he is abashed, needy; then, after this stripping, after he has been shrunk to silence, he is given an image to pursue in his emptiness, an erotic heuristic.

. . .

Socrates responds with incredulity to Diotima's claim that eros is universal, part of the quixotic effort of mortal nature to be forever; this appetite-driven exigency for immortality, she says, governs everything from animal sexual activity to the study habits of human beings (207d–208b). But after this eruption, we hear nothing further from him. Socrates is silent during Diotima's long disquisition on the spiritual progeny of eros that precedes the perfect revelations of erotics, silent, too, throughout her later revelations. Socrates's silence is remarkable because many of Diotima's observations before she embarks on her description of eros's ascent seem counterintuitive. She speaks, for instance, of a pregnancy of soul—she adumbrates an erotics of interiority—that is preferable to physical pregnancy. The issue of these pregnancies, which are brought to term by contact with an arresting, generous soul, are virtues, poetry, and law. These provoke the admiration of all because they engender every sort of decency (209e). And so people erect monuments only to the just, poets, and jurists. How to account for the odd equivalency of virtue, literature (poetry in particular), and law? The three appear to occupy different phyla. And how do these activities sprout virtue? Diotima mentions this last thing as if it happened with the inevitability of scientific law.

There is no resemblance among these three things except that each of the offspring of spiritual pregnancies appears to act as a paradigm for behaviour, enticing it, shaping it: they achieve this by arousing admiration. One explanation for Socrates's silence in the later part of Diotima's pre-ascent remarks is that he indeed has become transfixed by the aptness of what she proposes—she gives him something that holds his gaze and resists interpretation, something that seems outlandish yet intimate. Socrates learns nothing from Diotima, but he is altered. Here an Agathon-like attachment to physical beauty, underwritten by a belief in a beautiful god, is edged aside by a new capacity to discern and be drawn by something more hidden. He is disarmed, but collects no new information. To the list of the offspring of the pregnant soul, then, a fourth sort might be added: the speech of an erotic individual.

· · ·

Her lesser teachings on eros, Diotima tells Socrates, are a "means" to the perfect revelations "if one were to proceed correctly on the way" (210a). It is tempting to think that she means this gnostically, that she's claiming she has presented Socrates with a gleaming intellectual key to unlock the higher mysteries she is about to reveal, or a model that replicates them, a propadeutic of some sort to a more esoteric understanding. But what Diotima has said is incoherent as system: eros is a magician, a druggist, a sophist, a servant of Aphrodite, a priest (203a), a hunter, the bastard child of a god, a philosopher (203d). She says almost too much. The variety of identifications edges toward randomness; if one scans her remarks for knowledge about eros, an accurate replication of desire in thought, one comes up with nothing, each epithet — eros is a hunter of beauty, is a servant of beauty — cancelling another. The lesser revelations of eros, it is important to remember, are the speech of someone sufficiently erotic to initiate another in eros, and who therefore philosophizes as eros does: Diotima's remarks lie, then, between wisdom and lack of understanding and their substance is the altering effect they have on the interlocutor — here it is the effacing of Socrates's youthful erotic piety that resembles his own later demolition of Agathon's delicate encomium to desire. What Diotima's teaching points to is eros as the awareness of one's persistent poverty, and an attempt to rectify this by reaching for things, by seeking to be brought to such things that are adamantly distant, ungainsayably beloved, to be brought into the company of things that are unassimilably beautiful. And in this pointing, Diotima's lesser revelations have a psychagogic rather than a scientific effect: they do not reveal the nature of a force but hasten a participation in it.

The erotic life, the philosophic life, begins properly when someone who is young goes "to beautiful bodies" (210a), Diotima's higher revelations unremarkably begin;

then, guided correctly, the one-who-would-be-wise must be induced to love a single body, and in the company of this individual experience the generation of "beautiful speeches." Then he must be brought to the realization that the beauty of this particular body, the object of his devotion, is really the same as the beauty of all beautiful bodies; there is only a single form of physical beauty, he must be made to see, and it is petty for him to focus his erotic intentions upon one person; he will feel contempt now for his frenzied misapprehension and will slacken his pinpointed, amorous intensity. Next he must come to believe that the beauty in souls is superior to the body's comeliness, so that even if the beloved has only "a slight youthful charm" but a decent soul, he, the lover, will be satisfied with him (210c), and, generating beautiful speeches that will improve his young beloved, he, the older lover, will experience a compulsion to consider the beauty found in activities and laws. This will serve to deepen his conviction concerning the triviality of physical beauty. Then the lover must lead his beloved, the beautiful, charming young man, to consider the sciences, so that he, the lover, may note himself the beauty the sciences contain, a vast beauty he will be drawn to look on. Here the lover will undergo a conversion: he will make a "permanent turn" to "the vast open sea of the beautiful" that his attention to the sciences will expose, giving birth "in ungrudging philosophy" to even more beautiful speeches and thoughts (210d); here he will set aside the slavish attention to the beloved, the typical devotional stance of lovers, will cease to be a "petty calculator" in matters of love. He will turn away from the beloved, stand in some sort of apartness, and "increased" will make out a particular form of philosophical science the object of which is something surpassingly beautiful, complete and invariant, universally drawing, singular, the root of all other beautiful things (211b), young men, bodies, activities, laws, sciences. The intensity, the zeal that the apperception of "the beautiful itself" arouses will be like the self-abnegating excitement the sight of the beautiful beloved provoked but more profound: the one who has had this sight will wish always to behold it, be with it, neither eating nor drinking if necessary. In this contemplation, he will give birth to true virtue, become dear to the god, and, perhaps, be made immortal.

It is difficult to see how truly odd Diotima's revelations are because her remarks historically have been interpreted often as a program for the spiritualization of desire, a ladder of perfection, as the titles of so many medieval treatises on the interior life put it. But Diotima herself says her account is nothing other than a detailing of "the correct practice of pederasty" (210e, 211c); she insists that philosophy is the result of a complete sifting of the amorous involvement of an older man with an attractive young man: the way of eros, the way of philosophy, is an ascesis conducted in the context of such a relationship, in the end abandoned, in which the lover leads the beloved while still being drawn by him, yet is guided himself over all by an unnamed guide. This involvement benefits the beloved—he becomes "better"—yet chiefly rewards the lover who, in striving, becomes dear to the divine and is offered whatever sort of deathlessness a mortal may be granted. The relationship, in all of its transmogrifications, is marked by zeal, the very quality that Diotima hopes will distinguish her revelations; it breeds and fosters the wanting of one thing, though the nature of this single thing shifts. It is a kind of madness, a being swept along, where the lover, correctly guided, is presented with a series of objects of longing, which before did not compel him, but which now lift him utterly from himself. The unfolding appears to proceed with scientific inevitability.

The maieutic significance of Diotima's remarks is paramount; she is teaching Socrates — endeavouring, that is, to alter him — after all, not seeking to add to his store of knowledge on the erotic life. Her perfect revelations are neutral on the matter of ontology; she makes no claims about the nature of the psyche, even though she insists on the universality of eros; there is no necessity in this particular unfolding of desire, though, in retrospect, it may appear providentially to bear the signature of a luminous inevitability. Further, the maieutic significance of the ascent of desire is double: Diotima traces it for Socrates and Socrates repeats her account to his dinner companions: Socrates's story about his instruction from Diotima continues his refutation of Agathon. The psychagogic import of the image of the lover moving from one sort of desire to another is crucial in Diotima's use of it with Socrates and Socrates's reuse of it with Agathon.

Diotima's ascent story offers a taxonomy of lovers that is like the taxonomy of souls Socrates presents to the young Glaucon in books eight and nine of the *Republic*; it is an extended thought experiment proposed to Socrates in which he participates imaginatively in a number of discreet desires, assuming in this a series of interior dispositions, some of which — perhaps especially the earlier sexual ones — will seem strange to him. Diotima's descriptions of the various erotic conditions are necessarily brief: their object is the activation of her interlocutor's imagination, not the articulation of an erotic doctrine. The shortness of her account, and the quick changes that occur within it that bring speed — zeal, the Dionysiac element — to her telling, encourage Socrates to practise in imagination the erotic absorption into which she wishes to initiate him. Her whole description of erotic ascent is an elongated form of linguistic rapture like Socrates's period of abstraction in the doorway that delayed his arrival at dinner and the transport of intellectual ecstasy Alcibiades later describes him undergoing during the campaign at Potidaea (220c). More: as Socrates interiorly participates in these erotic states absorbedly, he uses them up, and so comes to experience the moment in each stage when the beloved ceases to be the beloved, no longer calls, where each place confesses its deficit. And, savouring this in his imagination, he experiences the craning of hybristic self-regard that will reach further. It is true that part of the imperative in the ascent account, the exigency forcing erotic change, is the insistence of the guide, charged with keeping the lover "correctly on the way," but also what provides movement is such hybristic appetite, reaching past the present lover to a more compelling love, this done out of an experience of poverty, this nevertheless drawing the superseded loves along. The erotic transmogrifications Socrates enacts in his imagination at Diotima's bidding are a building, not an enervation, of desire, coming to the desire for all things in the desire for the beauty in which all things "share" without its being diminished or augmented (211b), a beauty that is total, that never tests belief in itself (211a), that is apart, nonarticulable, unstudiable (211a). By attending to this without comprehension, its complete gracefulness, one becomes it; one is taken over by what it is. An adoption occurs at the end of pursuit, and this quickens true virtue (212a). Socrates, having rehearsed the schema, is enraptured by it, placing his life in its form, honouring erotics and training himself "exceptionally" in them (212b), by re-enacting them interiorly as he does when he reports them to Agathon and the rest, urging them on others by practising their enthusiasms and alterations with acquaintances as we soon learn he has done with the young, outlandishly gorgeous Alcibiades.

. . .

The form of Alcibiades's eruptive speech that ends the dialogue is the same as Socrates's: he reports the erotic conversion he has undergone with his teacher, although unlike Socrates he has not experienced a refutation and ravishment but the "outrage" of being deprived of his sustaining confidence in his own attractiveness (222b). Nevertheless, like Socrates before him, he has been disarmed and drawn disconcertingly to a beauty he had not known before. He enters Agathon's courtyard at the end of the festivities as Dionysus himself, crowned with the ivy and violets of the god, drunk and shouting, accompanied by flute players, in a roaring, imperious state of bacchic possession, haranguing the others at the party for their sobriety: he soon has them drinking from the wine cooler itself, eight pints altogether at once, he the self-declared new leader of the drinking. He has come to crown Agathon for his victory in poetry, he says, but he does this with half a heart: like Socrates, he had been absent from Agathon's euphoric victory celebration the previous day. Alcibiades then sees Socrates and begins to unwind the wreathe he has just placed on Agathon in order to crown him who "conquers all human beings with speeches, not just the day before yesterday... but at all times" (213e). There is no question who the favourite of the god is. The others have received Socrates's remarks on eros with little comment; the speech has summoned Dionysus himself to bestow on its maker the marks of victory, made by stripping apart Agathon's crown; here is a divine recognition equalling the Pythia's declaration in favour of the wisdom of Socrates reported in the *Apology*.

Eryximachus tells Alcibiades he must give an address eulogizing eros if he is to enter the spirit of the party. As an erotic individual, he is incapable of such a formal account of what drives him; he elects to praise Socrates instead, saying he fears hybristic revenge if he praises anyone else in his presence; besides, Alcibiades admits the equivalency between eros and Socrates without hesitation. He praises him, however, by comparing him to Dionysiac figures, sileni and the satyr Marsyas, whose flute playing, which has a divine source, causes possession and reveals "those who are in need of the gods and initiatory rituals" (215e). The possession that Socrates causes is comparable, but his music—the music of philosophy—is made with plain words without instruments. Socrates is more than Dionysiac, however; the god himself does him homage: eros—philosophy—includes and extends bacchic frenzy. While Marsyas challenges Apollo to a musical duel, loses, and is flayed, Socrates is acquiescent to divine things, going "where the god is leading" (Crito 54e); his is the alert, appetitive, noncontentious passivity of the erotic individual.

The lover is the favoured person in Diotima's account of erotic ascent; Alcibiades, in tracing his botched seduction of Socrates—he tries repeatedly to draw him to his bed—tells the same story from the perspective of the beloved. It is an account of an upending where the Socratic lover overshadows the muscular beauty of the beloved with an interior beauty of his own; Alcibiades complains he's not the only victim of such treatment: Charmides, Euthydemus, and others have experienced such reversal and found themselves entrapped in the eros of philosophy (222b). Alcibiades is ravished by Socrates's speeches and Socrates's true, hidden identity as the beloved is surfaced; though homely accounts about pack-asses and blacksmiths, Socrates's words have an unusual "sense inside" that arouses Alcibiades's moral imagination, exercising all his interior senses: he has seen something "golden" and been drawn (217a). "Bitten and struck," snakebit, by what Socrates has said, he himself is in the erotic life; electrified, thrust into himself, ashamed (216d), he is engaged, as he tells the story of his disarming love, in doing philosophy, though he soon will exile himself from the practice.

II

Three

HOW CASSIAN READ

Totus in lectione, totus in oratione

JOHN Cassian's *Conferences* lastingly introduced thought about longing as noesis to Europe. It was Western monasticism's originary book; from it rose that small, durable home for the attentive heart: the *Rule of St. Benedict*. In Cassian's book, desire is amplified, drawn by reading: reading brings wanting the large good of the emotional scent of a final cause; and the persistent gravity this telos works on desire pulls it to shapeliness. All forms of anagogic reading in *Conferences*—*lectio divina*, hesychastic repetition, *opus Dei*—depend on a desire that must precede them, the same desire they subsequently will form—specifically the poverty within this desire. Humility is the means by which reading in Cassian is rescued from a seamless exegesis and an ontology that in their urge to completeness increase one's separation from the nourishment within what one reads—this separation *superbia's* balm, *superbia's* wound—and turns one "to the lore which illuminates through the achievement of love" (*Conferences* 14. 10. 11), the erotic knowing of comingling.

. . .

Certain forms of literature, Origen observed, are like human beings—they are tripartite, with bodies, souls, and spirits (*On First Principles* 4. 2. 4). All psychagogic books, scripture pre-eminently, but also secular works like Hermas's *The Shepherd*, he says, possess such strata, thus have interior lives. The latter two meanings are hidden, the first lightly, the second profoundly, and are reachable only through an ascetical practice that has not been formed by the deeper readings, but that the deeper readings, when reached, alone will fully augment. To be grasped by these meanings and be altered— impossible to come to this by interpretation, impossible by ontologically inspired inquiry—is to be understood by oneself, to enter, by reading's anagoge, the other world beside this world, the place of stretching intelligibility. The second reading pulls to virtue—and in it reason bears an impressive load; the third to contemplation—perhaps over the objections of understanding.

Books are psychagogic when lifted in the wake of philosophical practice, when they are, in other words, daimonic, infused. But they must be incidental to this practice, accidents; when they are intended as transformative, they are sophistry.

If the writer, that is, is not helpless in the work, erotic yet passive, helpless but alert, she or he is a sophist. One contrarily disposed, ignorant yet drawn, alone would be able to mount an argument that their work was of scant consequence (*Phaedrus* 278 c–d).

. . .

The contemplative life rises from language, but the forms of reading Cassian recommends are peculiar: here reading's intent is not analytic, taxonomic, hermeneutic, but maieutic: understanding, always burgeoning, is the transformed life. A later account of this understanding is never systematic, can hardly be written: the altered life is the sole, complete figure for an otherwise nonreportable approach to what reason has been ravished by and loves. Less complete accounts may exist in poetry or in anamnetic literature like apothegmata, or, equally, in the dialogues of Plato, but these are partial, more heuristic than description.

Prayer, says Cassian, is the plain attention within the "regular reading and continuous meditation on Scripture"; such reading, *lectio divina*, is not palliative, not distraction, but an inquiring probe into what draws but cannot be said. It is the push of besotted reason toward what it senses, almost as a fragrance (*Conf.* 1. 1. 2), yet cannot know; but its aim is chiefly ascetical: one reads this way "so that a spiritual turn may be given to memory" (*Conf.* 1.17. 2). Or further: prayer is the unbroken repetition of a single psalmic verse,

Psalm 70: 1, for instance; you turn this over repeatedly
within and so "lift yourself upward": this ceaseless facing of
a model is training, the mind raised by the muscle of hesychasm (Conf. 10. 10. 1). Cassianic prayer, lastly, is *opus Dei*, the
discipline of psalmody, the regular singing of psalms, read
or recited from memory, meant to engender an implacable
compunction, the mind's slimming (Conf. 1. 17. 2).

Cassian's notion of reading says that writing with formative power has a subterranean vitality that scarcely shows
on the surface of writing—a shadow book lies within the
book, hidden—and that one gains entry to this altering,
inner book through forms of attention, ways of holding language before one, which themselves provoke the same sort
of change in the reader that the sequestered force within
writing later will with even greater power. Such reading is an
ascesis; such reading is a lifting. One does not read for comprehension but to be made comprehensible, trued. Each of
these forms of attention to literature, to writing with its own
interiority, exercises, as well, a suppressant effect on imagination, and so helps to produce, says Cassian, *puritas cordis*, a
pure heart, the treasure of the contemplative life: each nar-
rows and sustainingly builds desire.

So attention to language in Cassian is paideia; true reading
works as a lever on the reader, this reading also a disorientation, an intoxication. Cassian's instructions for reading are a
theological *poiesis*, which are also an account of love resting
on one thing, then building: comprehension may or may not
be coincident with this. Whether this comprehension is

great or small is of secondary importance; however, greater comprehension entails a greater temptation by theory. But it would be wrong to see anti-intellectualism in Cassian's ascesis of reading.

· · ·

Evagrius Ponticus, the chief philosopher in Egyptian monasticism, was the child of a chorbishop, Palladius reports in the *Lausiac History*, a minor, rural, itinerant hierarch, exercising limited episcopal powers under a metropolitan. He was raised near the family estate of Basil the Great, where a monastic community recently had been established that was to shape life in Cappadocia and monasticism throughout the eastern Mediterranean. Evagrius was ordained a lector by Basil, and later, in 379, a deacon by Gregory of Nazianzen, a colleague of Basil, who was soon to be appointed bishop in the imperial see at Constantinople, where he was charged with meeting the threat of Arianism, which had won over large numbers of people, including members of the emperor's immediate family. Evagrius, following his mentor to Constantinople, proved to be an illustrious disputant for the Nicean side; he rose to prominence as the orthodox cause grew in popularity in the city.

Evagrius fell in love with the wife of an important official during these years of celebrity and left Asia Minor for Jerusalem as a result, where he lived in the community of Melania, a wealthy Roman widow, on the Mount of Olives.

Melania and her friend Rufinus were ardent readers of
Origen—Origen comes into Latin through Rufinus's translation; Melania, Palladius records, turned night into day
reading him[1]—and supporters of Egyptian monasticism
even before Melania's visit to the cells of Nitria in the early
370s. Likely because of her influence, Evagrius spent the rest
of his life in various monastic communities south of
Alexandria; through him, the influence of Origen grew large
in the desert.

Evagrian epistemology is largely ascesis: the subjugation
of "thoughts" (*Praktikos* 6) breeds impeturbability: with this
emptiness, knowing occurs. The goal of *praktike*, spiritual
exercise, Evagrius remarks in *Gnostikos*, is "to purify the
intellect and render it impassible" (*Gnostikos* 49): knowing
depends upon a chastening of the self, a quelling of the flick-
ering movement of the self; it is what happens when the
athletic, striven-for stillness appears. He takes the notion of
praktike from Gregory of Nazianzen, who used it to describe
the life of bishops, and tilts it, sharpening it to apply to the
contemplative life in general, to the monastic life in particular. *Praktike* is what Christianity is, along with *theoria physike*,
contemplation of the physical world, and *theologia*, contemplation of divinity (*Pr.* 1): the kingdom of heaven is emptiness
of soul, apatheia, permeability—and "true knowledge of
existing things" (*Pr.* 2). This interior state of spreading quiet
has a single offspring, *agape*, which is the sole doorkeeper to
deep knowledge of being, the apprehension of things
denuded of the additions of attachment.

Apatheia, the soul's health, is the evacuation of images from keen, numinous attention (*Pr.* 65); this imagelessness is the end of the Evagrian therapeutics of "thoughts," the eight misdirections capable of stirring the passions, blocking attention, truncating eros itself—gluttony, impurity, avarice, sadness, anger, acedia, vainglory, and pride (*Pr.* 6)—all plausible, febrile, enervating.

Avarice, for instance, "suggests to the mind a lengthy old age, inability to perform manual labour (at some future date), famines that are sure to come, sickness that will visit us, the pinch of poverty, the great shame that comes from accepting the necessities of life from others" (*Pr.* 9). This "mother of idolatry" is met, Evagrius says, by stability, a canny staying where one is; the conflict itself is psychagogic: to flee it "schools the spirit in awkwardness, cowardice and fear" (*Pr.* 28). Here, as elsewhere, Evagrian psychagogery heals at a slant. The balm for sadness is inching from pleasure (*Pr.* 19); anger is disarmed by singing the psalms and almsgiving (*Pr.* 15). Anachoresis, turning within, the yielding of withdrawal, wrestles all demons (*Pr.* 52); reading wrestles all demons. Waiting during the time of sleep and prayer brings stability (*Pr.* 15).

Acedia—listlessness, restlessness, an itch for fleet rootlessness—is the least tractable menace, the last to be expelled (*Pr.* 12). Evagrius advises a practice of supposing one will die tomorrow in order to meet it; similar counsel appears in apothegmata associated with Antony and in Epictetus. No other seduction follows acedia; behind it comes the noetic emptiness of apatheia, and behind this, love appears: then one sees the world as it is. For Evagrius, the discipline involved in achieving *ordinatio caritatis*, ordered love, is the structure of true knowing.

· · ·

Totus in lectione, totus in oratione: the whole person in reading, the whole person in prayer: reading is reading's transformation; reading is prayer; comprehension is a turning; attention is a turning. Reading of a certain sort speeds permeability: that is, it breeds emptiness. Reading is ascetical, it is psychagogic. But not all reading is so — only what is anagogic, and not all works permit such reading: only those that have been infiltrated by ascetical practice, only those pushed up by erotic, philosophical momentum. The turn of anagoge is not being moved, is not inspiration; it is not a gestalt shift; it is not growth in erudition or understanding of any sort; it is not conversion; it can give no complete account of where it ends: it is a noetic blindness that is subverted by light; it is an interior posture that fruits out from a life-wide, persistent attention directed toward what arrests reason but that reason cannot say.

The rational part of the soul, in Evagrius's anthropology, recovers from its wounds once appetite reaches for the medicine of interiority (*Pr.* 85), which is virtue; once irascibility shifts into courage and patience as it enters combat with the daimons, then reason is brought back to its nature and fixes itself to the contemplation of "created things" (*Pr.* 86).

Apatheia in the rational soul, virtue in reason, appears as prudence, understanding, and wisdom (*Pr.* 89); as the latter, it is never stably settled, though it approaches asymptotically true gnosis of being (*Pr.* 87).[2] Virtue's issue, its necessary issue, grain from seeds, is knowing (*Pr.* 90); reading is a work that is a prerequisite fashioning that builds to this knowing.

. . . .

John Cassian was a Scythian, native of the Dobrudja, present-day Romania. He went to Egypt in 385 from a monastery near the cave of the nativity at Bethlehem, in search of "perfection," travelling with a friend, his fellow countryman Germanus; both men were convinced they had been ill-equipped for a life of desert solitude by their short period in the cenobium (*Conf.* 19. 11. 1). Each promised a return to their original community, and each later broke this promise; they were looking for teachers. They made a landfall at Thennesus near the Nile's eastern mouth, and, helped by Bishop Archebius of Panephysis, a former hermit pressed into episcopal office, were introduced to a community of solitaries living in the salt marshes in the river's delta (*Conf.* 11–18); later Cassian and Germanus joined a second congregation of hermits in the desert of Skete (*Conf.* 1–10), under the leadership of Paphnutius, whom Palladius identifies as an Origenist. While there is no record of Cassian having been taught by Evagrius, Evagrius was the leading synthesizer of Origen and Egyptian monasticism in the desert, and few non-Coptic monks failed to come under his influence—Cassian's preference for imageless prayer, for instance, is clearly Evagrian.

In 399, Theophilus, bishop of Alexandria, issued a customary letter shortly after Epiphany in which he set the dates for Lent and Easter; the letter went on to denounce "the foolish heresy of the anthropomorphites" (*Conf.* 10. 11. 2). Cassian reports that this denunciation was received with "great bitterness" by most of the monks; none of the presbyters in Skete, aside from Paphnutius, agreed to have it read in their churches. The outraged monks accused the bishop himself of heresy and stormed Alexandria, where they rioted. Theophilus met the crowd and initially upheld the argument of his letter—that God could not be imagined as having a human form—but then reversed himself, condemning what the rebellious monks called "Origenism." This reversal began the chain of events that led to the expulsion of all monks under the influence of Evagrius—chiefly Greek- and Latin-speaking foreigners—from Egypt. This expulsion included Cassian, who next appeared as a newly ordained deacon in Constantinople in 403, under the authority of John Chrysostom.

Cassian reports Theophilus's letter, and Paphnutius's support of it, with approval: rustic naïveté, he says, has caused the Coptic monks, most of whom were illiterate, to misconstrue the Genesis description of the making of man in the likeness of God in crudely physical anthropomorphic terms, and to employ such an anthropomorphically angled imagination in prayer. The purest form of prayer, he has the elder Isaac say in response to the crisis, will "permit itself neither the memory of any word whatsoever, nor the likeness of any deed, nor a shape of any kind" (*Conf.* 10. 5. 3). Here is the mark of Evagrius: prayer should be "free from all matter," an unrepresented knowing gained by drawing near "the immaterial Being" (*Chapters on Prayer* 66).

Not only is Evagrian prayer empty, but it is also termless (*Pr.* 87), a sustained posture of erotic availability—even though the subduing of the passions, the object of ascetical theology, he believed, had an end, as did *theoria physike*, the contemplation of nature. The contemplation of the Trinity, however, was "unlimited" (*Gnos.* 4. 87–8), a borderless unknowing, a "silence" (*Gnos.* 41). Evagrius's notion of limitless contemplative striving resembles Gregory of Nyssa's teaching of epektasis: the pursuit of gnosis of divinity is by nature endless. Furthermore, not only is God incomprehensible, in Evagrius's view, but so, too, is the individual soul (*Gnos.* 3. 31), the one thing in nature able to receive the impress of the Trinity itself.

· · ·

The end of contemplative attention is purity of heart, says Cassian (*Conf.* 1. 5. 2., 1. 7. 1); this state is *theoria*, divine contemplation (1. 8. 2); it is the totality of what *philosophia* is; it resembles Socratic permeability. *Puritas cordis* is attentiveness; it alone is what builds attentiveness, what makes for being "one" (1. 8. 3). It begins with reflection "on a few holy persons," is then, a reading of the life of one who is able to read you, who is able readily to detect a lover. Cassian and Germanus, in the initial *Conference*, approach the old man Moses in the desert of Skete; his knowledge—"his practical and contemplative virtue"—strike them not as coherent system, but as perfume (1. 1. 2): they ask him for edifying instruction. He refuses to give them this at first, but at last is worn down by their pleading, their tearful pleading. Moses, however, does not act as a teacher out of charity: the penthic sadness and the eros (1. 1. 8) of the two draws his speech; without such conditions in his auditors, what he might say could not be other than boasting (1. 1), lightmindedness (10. 9. 3), a trap. The state of the listener can falsify speech with true gnosis, even for the speaker, can induce inarticulacy in the one who knows (1. 23. 2), can affect the true words so that they are a betrayal of "important things."

Purity of heart, Moses tells them, is perfection. Besides the ascesis of yielding to the "fragrance" of the contemplative individual, its "tools" are the horror of vast solitude (1. 2. 3); readings (1. 7. 1); vigils; fasts; being stripped of everything— honours, family, homeland (1. 6. 3). But the achievement of these—even the setting aside of magnificent properties, the impressed Cassian says—the athleticism of such acts, may yet leave one irritable over lesser losses, or besotted with the practice itself (1. 7. 4); reading may breed contempt for those near. The losses are ascetical theology only when undergone while the heart is fixed in pursuit of its proper end: its own erotic availability. Only when so narrowed may it feed on the beauty and *theoria* of divinity (1. 8. 3).

The emptiness of Cassian's pure heart is not interior immobility: it quivers with the intensity of the interior gaze (1. 12. 1); it is not impassibility: it is the most erotic of states in which the mind's attention is fixed unceasingly on Christ, where the smallest interruption of the gaze is "fornication" (1. 8. 1). Nor is it actual Evagrian emptiness: *puritas cordis* does not involve cessation of thoughts (1. 18. 2); thoughts rise but the mind is smoothed by diaeresis, counterfeits set apart from *obrizim*, purest gold (1. 20. 1), so that one becomes a single act or thought — an unbroken interior looking. The source of discernment is reading, "the frequent reading of and medita-tion on Scripture," which quickens compunction, gathering the mind stretched to its limits (1. 17. 2): reading as sorrow, reading as the simplification, the intensification of desire.

. . .

The book was an object of sharp emotional interest in the desert. An apothegmatum concerning the abba Anastasius recalls he owned a single volume, written on very fine parch-ment, worth eighteen pence, containing both the Old and New Testaments. A visiting monk saw the magnificent book and took it, intending to sell it later in the city for sixteen pence. His buyer, however, was suspicious, and brought the book to Anastasius for it to be evaluated. Assured by the abba that it was worth at least this much, the buyer returned to the city to complete the transaction, but the monk who had stolen the book, hearing that Anastasius had done nothing but praise the quality of the book, now refused to sell it, and returned, instead, stricken, to the abba. Anastasius declined to take the book back, offering it now to the thief as a gift. The monk stayed with the abba the rest of his days.[3]

Anastasius's detachment from this book on fine parchment is offered as proof of surpassing sanctity: books were charged physical presences in the desert, the last test, because of the centrality of exegesis in monastic practice. All of the theorists of desert prayer, Origen, Evagrius, John Cassian, held that mystical understanding grew from the exercise of certain sorts of reading. Origen's mystical theology is entirely exegetical: it is indistinguishable from the act of taking in a text. The mystical life is an injury suffered from sifting the Word, he says, an injury that is in fact the rising of desire. When one savours the sinuousness of all things brought out of the Logos, Origen observes, he will be pierced by a "chosen dart," and will "suffer from the dart Himself a saving wound" (Prologue to the *Commentary on the Song of Songs* 2). This home-bringing wound, which Origen also calls *vulnus amoris*, the wound of love, the love of the inner person, the wound which is the soul approaching its clearest form "under the stimulus of love's desire" (the Prol. 1), is eros woken by the Word. The point of reading is this standing-forth of eros: reading quickens the appearance of God who is desire in the one who reads (the Prol. 2, 1 John:4–7). Let the soul say: I have been wounded by Charity, Origen counsels in his long reading of the *Canticle of Canticles*; let it say: I have been pierced by "the loveworthy spear of his knowledge" (*Commentary on the Song of Songs* ii. 8); here is interior sensuality taught to speak by reading, a sensual mindedness that is in large part the words one reads anagogically fully assimilated.

Knowledge of the philosophic working of desire, Origen claims, begins with Solomon; from him, it passes to the Greeks. This knowledge is laid out in three books, Proverbs, Ecclesiastes, and the Song of Songs itself, each book corresponding to a particular ascesis of knowing—ethics, physics, and enoptics—that also may be called, according to Origen, the moral, natural, and inspective disciplines (the Prol. 3). The moral "inculcates a seemly manner," an inclination to right reason; the natural gives knowledge of things so that nothing may be done that is contrary to nature; the inspective shapes in the soul a craning for divine things (the Prol. 3). All amount to the correction, the lifting of desire, so that it claims the power of vivification; all achieve their ends when the words of scripture are "stretched out" in the heart (Prov. 1:24, the Prol. 3), expanding the things first said enigmatically. The highest form of reading, anagogy, lifts, enlarges, confounds, changes, brings one to oneself. It is a heeding flavoured with a faithful anticipation; such reading may be a hearing of harmony ("God's music") within what appears to be discord: it may leave the understanding "unfruitful," even as it feeds the range of faculties aiding the soul—"believe," says Origen, "that thy soul is profited by the mere reading," even though the "understanding does not receive the fruit of the profit from these passages." The inner nature, meanwhile, is charmed as an asp under the spell of the charmer.[4]

It is charmed as if it is remembering, or being remembered through, as if the "immense, monstrous animal" of the universe (*On First Principles* 2. 1. 3), in unstable dispersion, feels out the shape of its unitary girth. Through catanyxis, ascesis, attention, each powered by desire, the scattered, unselfconscious oneness remembers itself; the contemplative remembers herself as unlike, pulled, recalls a fuller extent, false dawn, then dawn, revealing a complete terrain; remembering is return and identity in union, "bending the knee at the name of Jesus" (1. 6. 2; Phil. 2:10), each one recognizing itself—and all near it—in the dislocation into the otherness, the strangeness of beauty. Here knowing is a "whirling" (1. 8. 4), is a "wavering" (1. 8. 4), a "tossing" (2. 1. 1), a "winding" (4. 4. 10), the soul running "round God" "since it cannot go to him."[5] The various momentumed, shifting states of being are psychic states, fallennesses, yet also stations—understandings, lives, "nations," each a *mundus imaginalis*—in the spectacle of return, this passage to the end that is like the beginning the soul's inexorable school (1. 6. 2., 1. 6. 4., 3. 6. 3). Origen's epistemology is eschatological, and, like his theodicy, inseparable from cosmology. In reading, which is divine eros thinking through dissatisfaction (4. 3. 11), one lurches into one mind, where feeling, understanding, thinking "will all be God" (3. 6. 3), a region of unlikeness, "the treasures of darkness and riches hidden in secret places" (Isa. 45:3).

. . .

Prayer, in Evagrius, is knowing and ascesis; it is nourishment
to the intelligence as bread is to the body, as ordered desire is to
the soul (*Chapters on Prayer* 101); prayer drives out acedia's
despondency; the imagelessness of highest prayer can defeat a
sort of inner pomp (116). Prayer's knowledge is proximity and
decorum, not representation by analysis—and it is higher than
this latter knowing: "If you are a theologian you truly pray,"
says Evagrius. "If you truly pray you are a theologian" (60).
Prayer is the nature of the spirit working (*Praktikos* 49); it is the
"following of Christ" (*Chapters on Prayer*, Introductory Letter); it
is another mind and desire within one, these appearing as gifts
(58), provoking surprise, delight at aptness, gratitude.

Evagrius's instruction on prayer, offered to an unnamed
correspondent, perhaps Rufinus, is a random abundance,
rough-edged in overall shape, 153 remarks that, he says, came
to him after he had "worked the whole night through and...
caught nothing" (Introductory Letter); they are writing that
he presents as a "vehicle of the spirit," an anagogic device: he
invites his reader to set upon his observations as a dish.
Prayer, he says, rises from the virtues, "the highest act of the
intellect" (34), but does not inevitably rise from this place
(55); it is the likely, plausible flower of meekness, joy's bloom.
It begins best in penthos (5); it undermines sadness (16)—the
state of prayer, further, wakes discernment: it makes clear
the distinciton between sorrow and despair, and bestows an
appetite for the former. Indeed the atmosphere of prayer is

"respectful gravity," "coloured" by compunction (42). It is what appears when everything has been lost.

A late renunciation is the religious imagination—when you pray, Evagrius counsels, do not cast the divinity as an image within (66): such a move stirs the passion of vainglory; it is a rich grooming of the self; it is the demons attacking no longer "from the left side but from the right" (72), suggesting a likeness of God "flattering to the senses." Evagrius favours a patrolling of the spirit in prayer, keeping it free from concepts, ontological, theological, in deep, formless, anticipatory calm, an evacuated tending (67). A special solicitude for the self, a self-cosseting, "attempts to enclose the Divinity" in forms. The state of prayer is a "habitual state of impeturbable calm"; it is a snatching "to the heights of intelligible reality the spirit which loves wisdom," the spirit "truly spiritualized by the most intense love" (52).

Prayer is an ignorance (69), empty availability, erotic tracklessness, the portal for visitation—the end of reason's eros is visitation; reason arrives at last at fixed interior looking, looking and visitation. Poverty builds the stretching emptiness (130); affliction builds it; tears work toward it; plain attention seeks it: nothing else moves in the train of attention but prayer (149).

. . .

Origen fell under censure in matters of doctrine after the Origenist controversy erupted in Jerusalem in 393; Jerome, a former translator, turned on him, accusing him of heresy on matters of the fall of the angels, descent of the soul, the resurrection of deceivers, and the final redemption of all creatures (apokatastasis). In the same book, *Apologia adversus Libros Rufini*, Jerome also attacked, with justice, Rufinus, Origen's other translator in antiquity, for bringing an amended, de-Platonized Origen into Latin; even among the devoted there seem to have been doubts concerning the orthodoxy of Origen's ontology. Origen's exegetical style has been equally controversial throughout history. Luther's denunciation of his use of allegory is paradigmatic: meaning appears solely in the *simplici puraque et naturali significationi verborum*, the chastely simple and natural meanings of words[6]: further reading is caprice, a refusal to accept the sturdiness of the divine artifact of ordinary language. Later, nineteenth-century commentators criticized Origen's method as subjective, ahistorical; his hermeneutic employs no discernible method, is unscientific, a *jeu d'imagination*.

Origen's style of reading, it is true, is nonmethodological if method is coterminous with the practice of adding tested hypotheses together so that a range of probable claims is amassed; it is not objective, yielding a collection of facts. Nor is it analytic, but grows, instead, from an initially puzzled yet building attention; it is nonliteral, seeing the surface of writing as a place of imprisonment, "gates of brass" (*On First Principles* 4. 3. 11, Isa. 45:2), and wisdom as inevitably sequestered; it is subjective, but the result of an exercised, likely subjectivity that forms a paideia for the soul of a particular reader.

Origen offers a condensed version of his approach to reading at the beginning of Book IV of *On First Principles*— scripture is divine because it has daimonic effect: it alone achieves antiquity's ideal of teaching; it alone, that is, has power to cause its hearers to dedicatedly change their lives, provoking a return to nature; it, therefore, is the repository of *scientia* or truth (4. 1. 1). Later he makes an allowance for certain secular writings, such as Hermas's *The Shepherd*: these, too, contain "two books," one historical, the other, while in some sense incomprehensible, capable of speech to the awareness below the scree of thinking. Such books have knowledge, are *scientia*, this shown in their capacity to provoke and power an inner turning: they visit catanyxis and remodelling on readers; they trigger philosophy.

The route to the deeper readings, the "way" in the interior life (4. 22. 4), passes through ascesis and empty attention— both of which Cassian will later call purity of heart: they amount to singleness of gaze, the only cognition, in the Alexandrian hermeneutic, with penetrative power. Its method is simply wanting one thing, this moving unaccountably to spreading light, a method resembling the translation practice of the poet Paul Celan, who advised his own translators to simply, "Read! Just read again and again, the understanding comes by itself." For Origen, this penetrative reading is threefold, following the stages of the soul to perfection in the contemplative enterprise, an erotic itineracy (Prologue to the *Commentary on the Song of Songs* 1), the goal of which is a state of pure receptivity to divinity. The "flesh" of writing, its soul and its spirit, replicate the divine creative act of giving the individual first being, then reason, and finally sanctity (*On First Principles* 1. 3. 8); one must follow this same route in reverse in the practice of return—rapture, to reason, to divinisation, reading forming these states in the reader in whom desire is on the move, desire whose unfashioned, unwilled telos is restoration to an original resemblance to divinity (2. 11. 3).

. . .

Ceaseless prayer is the perfection of the single heart (*Conf.* 2. 1); it is desire's end, what makes desire strange and beneficent: the heart, too, by its nature, climbs toward unbroken tranquility, "perpetual purity"; for the sake of these, it walks toward "every bodily labour," walks toward compunction (9. 2. 1); one labours to virtue, that is, the end of that stickiness of mind that is wanting wrongly. This emptiness, lack of knowing—the passions always know precisely what is wanted—is the moment of purest eros, is when at last one can ingest contemplation's food (9. 3. 4). Here is where the soul, more itself than at any other time, is lightest, a bit of down, a "plume," liftable by the "slightest breath." Now interiority regains its natural suppleness, is weightless, available, subtle, taking the pose of shapely exigence; this is prayer as perpetual state, as returned nature; here eros penetrates "not only the heavens but even what is above the heavens" (9. 4. 3), seemingly without effort, from necessity, this action a remembered rhythmic habit. What is not nature is always heavy, relentless, wasting, "pounding a very hard rock with a sledgehammer," and it makes nothing: it is as if "another is with you whom you did not see," standing by, pressing the endeavour forward with compulsive force (9. 6. 3): the soul fattens, reels, and dithers (9. 5. 1). The empty mind, biddable longing, is not only unplucked by the passions, but also refuses with implacable strictness "those things that cater to our power and which have the appearance of a kind of goodness" (9. 6. 3); whatever it takes in, turns to, does now is purest prayer (9. 6. 5). *Puritas cordis* is the silence—intent, stretching—standing before the intelligibility, the speech, risibility, the eyed-ness of the world and what appears beyond it.

Cassian's erotics, his teachings on prayer, are heard, not assembled: they come to him in conversation with those whose subjectivity is plunging and capable of fostering diaresis. His thought on desire, then, is philosophic— Socratic—in content and grammar. His and Germanus's interlocutor in *Conference* 9, the first conference on prayer, is the abba Isaac, who knew Antony the Great and learned from the first monk's paradigmatic ecstasy (9. 31) that prayer is more than what the contemplative understands of himself and his prayer; that it is not uniform (9. 8. 2) or countable (9. 8. 1); that prayer is speech—supplication, vow-declaring, intercession, and thanksgiving—but beyond speech, "fiery," soundless eloquence of "purest vigour" (9. 15. 2); that it is liquefaction and familiar speaking (9. 18. 1), intelligence beyond the "self-conscious mind" (9. 25. 1). By it, the mind is "up-built" and "formed" (10. 6. 1) to an inward seeing of divinity, the image under view not anthropomorphic in impulse, not self-aggrandizing, apparently given; what aids such a gaze is "the support of withdrawal," anachoresis, "the benefit of the desert" (10. 6. 4); thus purity of heart is a fruit of where the body is placed: propadeutic to hearing is physical and social disloca-tion. The end of prayer is identity, the eros of God passing into the heart's single disposition, so that "[w]hatever we breathe, whatever we understand, whatever we speak may be God" (10. 7. 2).

This crescendo of Isaac's speech on prayer has a psych-agogic effect on his interlocutors: they are given an object for eros, the eros that is the reach for it and the poverty that is the means by which they will move forward: they are instructed, inflamed, shamed by their not knowing, struck by despair; they are made philosophic (10. 8. 1). Germanus now asks how one can assemble a bare beginning—what is the training, he inquires, in the erotic life that resembles the teaching of the alphabet to one who wishes to be instructed in grammar, thus acquiring "competence in rhetoric and philosophy" (10. 8. 3)? Isaac's response is, in fact, a disquisi-ton on *grammatica*, a theory of reading where understanding is becoming the text. Throughout the desert, even among the non-Origenist monks, some hermeneutic stood at the core of spiritual practice: the monastic work was to re-speak the language of scripture with the forms of one's life. But a trustworthy reading of these words depended on a prior ascetical formation—in silence, in withdrawal: to hear, you must be changed; hearing itself, too, can provoke a change that amounted to entry into a noesis of speechless comprehension. The reading that Isaac recommends, while possibly vocal, a physical activity, was a silence before the text, pressing, yet not reaching to interpretation, though devolving to practice—a hermeneutic of inarticulacy, ignorance, yearning, self-cultivation, worked out, in part, in hesychastic repetition of psalmic fragments.

How to manage a gathering of the heart's attentiveness, wonders Germanus (10. 8. 5). The question, Isaac remarks, shows that the one who asks it stands in the "vestibule" of purity, and this allows the teacher to speak with candor—without risk of light-mindedness—the formula for this spiritual *theoria* (10. 10. 1), what is absolutely necessary for perpetual awareness; that is, the gathering of the mind around the repetition of Psalm 70:1, "Be pleased, O God, to deliver me/O Lord, make haste to help me." The versicle, says Cassian through the abba, "takes up all the emotions…and… adjusts itself to every attack" (10. 10. 3); it hears, then, the heart more than the heart itself hears, and defends the heart with a fluid inventiveness, sharp-eyed, commodious; the writing hears the hearer and draws out what is latent. "It contains a burning love and charity, an awareness of traps, and a fear of enemies" (10. 10. 3). It repels acedia, repels despair; it disarms vainglory (10. 10. 10). Repeating the couplet without stint, one is shifted while held fixed in an impenetrable breastplate (10. 10. 3); one is given a retreat, making possible anachoresis, a breath-place; "you should write this on the thresholds and doors of your mouth" (10. 10. 15) and let it lead you to the *theoria* of invisibility (10. 10. 14).

This psalmic repetition crucially quells the imagination, blocking its wealthy, fifth-column consolations, while it speeds desire, blinding it, impoverishing it, giving it, thus, impressive range and commensurate durability (10. 11. 1). It strips one, and this emptiness draws the numinous near: language as abashment, language as a shrinking and raising. The psalm becomes the mind, and the mind goes ahead of comprehension: then one's inner postures become one's own teachers.

> For divine Scripture is clearer and its inmost organs, so to speak, are revealed to us when our experience not only perceives but even anticipates its thought, and the meanings of the words are disclosed to us not by exegesis but by proof. When we have the same disposition in our heart with which each psalm was sung or written down, then we shall become like its author, grasping its significance beforehand rather than afterward. That is we first take in the power of what is said, rather than the knowledge of it (10. 11. 5).
>
> Having been instructed in this way, with our dispositions for our teachers, we shall grasp this as something seen rather than heard, and from the inner disposition of the heart, we shall bring forth not only what has been committed to memory but what is inborn in the very nature of things (10.11.6).

. . .

Reading in psalmic hesychasm is an anagogic being-taken-over by writing, but elsewhere in Cassian, reading leads or drives up as well. Ascesis everywhere is the prelude to all knowledge, the single practice in which knowing appears (14. 2). It is thus the antechamber of reading, then reading's necessary attendant, reading's modifier, vivifier, without which reading shrinks to the surface of writing and knowledge to incoherent conviction. Deeper reading is impossible without moral practice; this deeper reading is itself a later ascesis, leading to a memorization of the text—the whole of scripture, says Nesteros in *Conference* 14—taking the work so into the mind that the mind becomes indistinguishable from the work, its postures transliterations into decorum of the work.

This knowledge that is religious life, the erotic life, for Cassian, is both practical and contemplative; the former noesis is twofold: a penetration, a setting into the light, of the nature of the misdirection of each passion—and a subsequent distancing from the power of each—and its slantwise remedy: anger, as with Evagrius, is broken down by almsgiving and psalmic singing. The second part of practical knowledge is picking out the sequence, the watercourse (14. 13. 5) of the virtues; his succession is not "guesswork" but a recognition of a causal series among the perfections that is not acquiesced to in obedience but is enjoyed as a severe, natural good (14. 3. 1)—this knowledge accessible in a range of situations, solitude, hospitality, care of the cenobium; all that is required is stability in the work undertaken (14. 15. 1). Silence and an attentive heart, says Cassian's Nesteros, are the beginning of practical discipline, intellectual humility, taking in what is given, not to master it but to "preserve" it in the contemplative gaze.

Contemplative work is *lectio divina,* and it, too, is "doubly clothed" (Prov. 31:24), split into historical interpretation, reading's surface, and spiritual understanding. The second knowledge is further divided into tropology, allegory, and anagogy; tropological reading directs interior correction; allegory, for Cassian, is prophetic; anagogy lifts the mind to a secrecy higher than what is highest (14. 8. 3), lifts it not into comprehension but clarified, directed appetite, beyond eristics (14. 16. 1), to the ability to be fed by what first confounds, and, by this lifting, the reading forms. All readings are part of a continuous, nonprogressing work that brings rest from the passions and a slackening of intention in which an unformed understanding grows (14. 11. 1), as definable as fragrance (14. 13. 5), working as a final cause on the heart.

. . .

Between 385 and 399, John Cassian witnessed extraordinary events—a new form of life being worked out at the limits of the empire and a new philosophy constructed that appeared to perfect the striving of the ancients—and he spent the rest of his life mulling over both, practising them and, after twenty years, writing about them at a length greater than he had intended (9. 1). The charge of what he had seen perdured; this durability was a mark for him of its daimonic nature. These collections of observations — perhaps in part pedagogical fictions flavoured by memory — together with Palladius's *Lausiac History* and other gatherings of apothegmata, served as the template for intentionality in Europe for the next twelve hundred years, until displaced by the strict empiricism, the dogmatic irreligion, of the new science. Cassian offered what he heard to the monks living on the Stoechadian Islands, southwest of Lerins, in the Rhone valley, to match and pull their sharp desire (Preface to *Conferences* XI–XVII. 2), and to save their abbot, Eucherius, from having to make the dangerous sea voyage to Egypt to read the acts of those still in the desert who had come through.

Four

KNOWING AS RITUAL

T HE *Divine Names* of pseudo-Dionysius the Areopagite begins with the word "and"; later, still in its initial clause, it mentions an earlier book, *The Theological Representations,* perhaps lost, perhaps fictional: *The Divine Names,* then, lies part way through a longer exchange between "Dionysius the Elder" and "Timothy the Fellow Elder" or presbyter.[1] Since it is addressed to an individual, the book is a work of spiritual direction, its cosmological complexity, the appearance of system throughout it, notwithstanding; it is a private instruction, that is, closer to oral communication than to a modern book of theological explanation. Its intent is the shaping of a particular soul—thus its repetitions, thus its inconsistencies—not the production of an exhaustive account of sacred nomenclature usable as doctrine, though the many names falling under its exegesis are in no way random.

The individual to whom the work is addressed is suited to a particular form of enlightenment, the one appropriate to his state of presbyter. In *The Ecclesiastical Hierarchy*, Dionysius explains that such a figure, as teacher, "has the understanding both to illuminate and to purify" (504A). The illumination peculiar to presbyters, "their powers of uplifting," and the enlightenment such ecclesiastics had the charism to bestow, is a form of contemplation, Dionysius says, which is an attention to divine symbols (*The Ecclesiastical Hierarchy* 532 B–C). The formation offered in *The Divine Names*, then, its particular "uplifting," is symbolic, undergone by means of a linguistic ritual.

The *Theological Representations* is summarized in Dionysius's *The Mystical Theology* (1032D–1033A) as a treatise of kataphatic theology, a theology of divine revelation, which is, in part, a disquisition on post-Nicene, post-Chalcedonic dogmatic theology, showing "the sense in which the divine and good nature is said to be triune"; how Fatherhood and Sonship are implicit in this nature. The book, as well, is a rendering of a theology of the Spirit and an account of the Incarnation, dwelling at length on Jesus who is both "above individual being" and a "being with a true human nature" (*The Mystical Theology* 1033A). Both *The Divine Names* and *The Theological Representations* are affirmative theologies, then, treatments of divinity insofar as it is knowable; both books are addressed to the same person: how, then, is the *via positiva* of the one to be distinguished from that of the other, since they appear to be parts of a single, ascending formation? The answer appears in the same review of a portion of the Dionysian corpus in *The Mystical Theology*: the kataphaticism of *The Theological Representations* is chiefly scriptural, while that of *The Divine Names* is "conceptual" (MT 1003A). The positive assertions in the first book rise from revelation and have a purifying effect (*The Ecclesiastical Hierarchy* 508B); those in *The Divine Names* come from human subjectivity alive to the sacral nature of being: their purpose is to enlighten and move.

The language of *The Divine Names*, the author reports in the second sentence of that treatise, is not intended to identify—an impossible project when the object of this exercise is divinity—but to lift the auditor: the author will "set down the truth 'not in plausible words of human wisdom but in demonstration of the power granted by the Spirit'" (1 Cor. 2:4); the language of the treatise is offered as force, then, "by which in a manner surpassing speech and knowledge, we reach a union superior to anything available to us by way of our abilities or activities in the realm of discourse or intellect" (*The Divine Names* 588A). It is the use of language that momentums its audience outside of language and discursive reasoning; its worth, like poetry's, is anagogic power: it jolts and alters vision. The alteration of perception, which is a deepening introspection, will be the path to union with the divine, being's cause, "[m]ind beyond mind, word beyond speech," which "is gathered up by no discourse, no intuition, by no name" (588A). But, like poetry, the language of *The*

Divine Names, while not explanatory, may not be capricious; this is praise, not ontology, but it aspires to be an actual mimesis, a hymnic noesis.

What is not named by this language is the "hidden transcendence of God" (588C), which is unreachable by any human power, unintuitable, unlovable, the fire that warms but that itself is not burnt (645D). Dionysius quotes Romans 11:33 on the intractable distance of divinity, the unqualified unsearchability of the Godhead—"there is not a trace for anyone who would reach through into the hidden depths of this infinity" (588C).

> It is at a total remove from every condition, movement, life, imagination, conjecture, name, discourse, thought, conception, being, rest, dwelling, unity, limit, infinity, the totality of existence (593C–D).

Yet this unknowability works "enlightenments proportionate to each being" (588A), which are not, in fact, satisfactions of the ambition to know all, including the vision of divinity, though the language seems to suggest this, but a drawing "to permitted contemplation, to participation and the state of becoming like it" (588D); this enlightenment is a raising "upward in the direction of the ray that enlightens them" (594A). One rises with an unconsoled eros, which is the totality of illumination: this rising is liturgical, the beings of those drawn formed by songs of praise (589B).

This praise, "revealing praises," names, but what is praised is not divine hiddenness, inaccessible even to delight, but "the beneficent procession of God" (589D). God in "procession," in the outflowing from unknowability that is first what dogmatic theology limns then all that is, is called "Trinity," a name that indicates fecundity; "cause"; "wise"; "beautiful"; "loving"—all the latter names, after the first revealed name addressed in *The Theological Representations*, are "conceptual": all the names in *The Divine Names*, in other words, are hailings, ejaculations, a cascade of apparent recognitions, which is hymnal, not taxonomic—yet, as with poetry, the names must be, in some way, true, for if they do not strike the one who uses them as apt, without being definitional, they will not seem suitable as praise.

The names shed light not on objects, not on divine states, but on subjective responses to what seems providential in being. They also possess anagogic strength, are, that is, subjective states concressed as language possessing the power themselves to transform interiority; they are "theurgic lights" (592B), into which one is initiated, "a tradition at one with scripture" (592B). The theurgic words are symbols: this identification with symbol in liturgical ritual or in the formative rite of reading, the rite exercised by *The Divine Names* itself, is introspection, wherein the soul, as Proclus remarked, "wants to enter within herself to see the circle and the triangle there, all things without parts in one another, to become one with what she sees" (*A Commentary on the First Book of Euclid's Elements* 141).

These "analogies"—names, symbola, geometric shapes, praises, ceremonial gestures—lift the reader (592C), strip all notions of the divine (592D), thereby disabling discursive thought, while leaving unmarred contemplative momentum.

. . .

Theurgy, ritualistic "god work," central to Neoplatonic philosophic practice, grew from Plotinus's use of metaphor in teaching; it also built from Plato's instructional tales. It achieved its fullest expression, though, in the work of Iamblichus in the third century. Theurgy's employment as a pedagogical device—an initiation into contemplative endeavour and an ascesis—rested in the ontological conviction that divinity was characterized equally by unity and differentiation (*The Divine Names* 640D–641A), with certain things peculiarly bearing the power to trigger memory of the origin of multiplicity in oneness—arithmetic and ritual objects for Iamblichus, geometrical forms and language for Proclus. These bore the deposit of divinity, the philosophers held, though they required a ritualistic liberation to be psychagogically useful. Iamblichus, in his *Life of Pythagoras*, praised the Pythagoreans' "marvellous divination and worship of the Gods according to the numbers most allied with them" (*Life of Pythagoras* 147). Proclus recommended the veneration of the sphere since it is "both itself one and capable of containing multiplicity, which indeed makes it truly divine, in that while not departing from its oneness, it dominates all the multiple" (*On the Timaeus* frag. 49, 27–9).

Such attention to number or form with sacred significance was meant to draw together the mind, initiating,
easing one into contemplation. As ascesis, it powered attention, attenuated attachment to discursivity, bestowed an
appetite for introspection. The most potent symbols have
the capacity to surprise and captivate, working in new pat-
terns of looking. Proclus, in *The Platonic Theology*, re-creates
the entire cosmos in language, gathering all its appropriate
names. He is not attempting natural science in this collection of hierarchies, he insists, not proposing a map of being,
but tracing the source of eccentricity in divinity, as he
observes in his *Commentary on Plato's Parmenides*, for formational ends.

So, as the *Timaeus* does not simply inquire about nature in
the usual manner of the natural scientist, but in so far as all
things get their cosmic ordering from the one Demiurge,
so also Parmenides, we may say, in conducting inquiry
about beings, is himself examining these beings in so far as
they are derived from the One (the Preface v. 641).

In Proclus's linguistic theurgic ceremony, a miniature of
being is assembled in the mind by an exegesis of Plato's dialogues, the *Parmenides* pre-eminently, which is a rehearsal of
the hierarchical structure in being, its object the creation of
an enlarged subjectivity, one formed by intimacy with divine
symmetry. Attention builds, tilting into adoration. Similarly,
the whole of Dionysius's *The Divine Names* is simultaneously

an exegesis, an ontology—angled so that it accommodates an anagogic reading—and a ritual.

. . .

The author of *The Divine Names* identified himself as one of a pair of prominent Athenian disciples of the apostle Paul mentioned in Acts 17:34; as a result, his work possessed what approached apostolic authority, short periods of doubt aside, into the sixteenth century. Thomas Aquinas cited him seventeen hundred times in his work; the Dionysian oeuvre formed the core of the philosophy curriculum at the University of Paris in the thirteenth century; but widespread skepticism about his identity appeared toward the end of the Middle Ages, and in 1520 Luther condemned him as a pernicious platonizer of unadulterated Christian thought.

The Pauline ministry to Athens was far from successful; in fact, it had not even been planned, but resulted from an earlier apostolic failure in Thessalonica, where a mob had driven the eristic evangelist from the city after he had caused dissension in the synagogue by fomenting an argument extending over three Sabbath days concerning the Messiah. The apostle's supporters in Thessalonica were forced to shift him and his assistant, Silas, to Beroea under cover of darkness; and, while his ministry in that place was less tumultuous, the Thessalonican Jewish community soon heard of his whereabouts and activities and sent emissaries to Beroea to "incite the crowds," causing Paul to be driven away again, by his supporters this time, to the Greek coast. Those charged with conducting him, however, took him only as far as Athens, where they abandoned him (Acts 17:15). There Paul was "deeply distressed" by the plethora of idols he found in the city, and proceeded, with typical ferocity, to remonstrate with individuals both in the synagogue and in the market-place on the matter of images; this drew the attention of certain Epicurean and Stoic philosophers, who, wondering "what this babbler wants to say," brought him to the Areopagus to give an account of his learning. Paul declared before his philosophical audience that "we are God's offspring," and denounced again the use of gold, silver, and stone images for the divnity. Further, he claimed, God had allotted the times of the existence of all beings and "the boundaries of where they would live," this an impetus to search for God "and perhaps to grope for him and find him" (Acts 17:27); the oration concluded with the claim that at the appointed time the world would be judged by a man who had been raised from the dead. Most of the Stoics and Epicureans balked at this last assertion, but a few remained attentive, "including Dionysius the Areopagite and a woman named Damaris."

Numerous figures have been proposed as the actual author of the *corpus dionysiacum*; some of these suggestions — Ammonius Saccas, the teacher of Plotinus, and Damascius, the last diadochus of the Academy in Athens — have been outlandish. The first notice of the Dionysian writings came in 532 in a report (*Innocenti Marionitae epistula de collatione cum Severianes habita*, "Epistle of Innocent the Marionite

Concerning a Conference Held with the Severians") of a theological exchange between orthodox followers of the Council
of Chalcedon (451), and its doctrine of the two wills of Christ,
and a group of disciples of Severus, who were Monophysites,
holding that Jesus, the incarnate Logos, possessed only a single, divine nature. This latter group advanced "Dionysius the
Areopagite" as an impeccable, patristic authority in support
of the heterodox position, along with the Alexandrians
Athanasius and Cyril. The Chalcedonian defenders rejected
the arguments of the Severians, discounting, in particular,
the support of Dionysius; such a figure, they argued, must
be spurious since no mention of him existed in the writings
of any prominent fourth-century theologian.[2] Innocent's
"Epistle" marks not only the earliest doubts concerning the
apostolic lineage of the Dionysian corpus, but also the onset
of uneasiness about its orthodoxy. Throughout the seventh
century, the Dionysian writings were associated with the
Monophysite and Nestorian cause, often lumped together
with the equally questionable doctrinal thought of Origen
and Evagrius. But with their translation into Latin in the
ninth century by John Scotus Eriugena, however, the writings won back most of their apostolic lustre.

While there has been considerable confusion over authorship, agreement has appeared concerning the date of the
composition of *The Divine Names, The Mystical Theology, The
Celestial Hierarchy,* and *The Ecclesiastical Hierarchy.* The last book,
a psychagogic account of liturgical conventions, mentions a
sung creed between the liturgy of the word and the liturgy of

the sacrament, a tradition introduced by Peter the Fuller, a Chalcedonian skeptic, in his second tenure as Patriarch of Antioch, 475–7.[3] "Dionysus," then, appears to have been a fifth-century Syrian. He was, thus, a late contemporary of Proclus (410–485), diadochus in Athens, whose methodological style — system as theurgy, exegesis as ascesis — is replicated in the Dionysian writings. While it might be tempting to suppose that the pseudonymity of the author of these works was meant to draw Pauline prestige to his position, it is more plausible, given the dissimilarity between Dionysian and Pauline thought, that it was intended to declare an entirely new way of thinking. He locates his authorship in Athens, in the midst of a fruitless philosophical conversation in which Paul of Tarsus, the self-proclaimed apostle to the Gentiles, makes various remarks that appear to echo Neoplatonic cosmology — God is the generative cause of all; being is a series of gradations or hierarchies; all beings "grope" toward God. Thus Dionysius announces a marriage of Christian revelation and Proclan ontology, to which Greek philosophy, represented here by curious Epicureans and Stoics, was unsympathetic, and of which Christianity proved soon to be suspicious on grounds of orthodoxy.

. . .

Eunapius, in his *Lives of the Sophists*, writes of the extraordinary theurgic practice of Maximus of Ephesus, a student of

Iamblichus and chief religious adviser to the anti-Christian emperor Julian. Maximus, Eunapius reports, was known to make the statue of the goddess Hecate smile, and to light from a distance the torches she held (*Lives of the Sophists* 7.2.7–12). Iamblichus himself performed equal feats, Eunapius continues, while Proclus, according to his biographer Marinus, received visions of Hecate, practised soothsaying by means of the tripod, and summoned oracles.

The ubiquity of such theurgic disciplines grew from the influence of *The Chaldean Oracles* on Neoplatonism from the third century onward. *The Oracles*, appearing in second-century Syria, purporting to be the speech of a medium in communication with the soul of Plato, claimed that all things possessed a symbol of divinity—this condition especially true of religious statuary, the *hermes*—and that interiority consisted largely in the liberation of this divinity through the manipulation and contemplation of such god-sequestering objects. Theurgy, the animation, vivification, illumination of daimonic figures, taught Proclus, was a valuable "intermediary," joining individuals to "the primordial causes," like love's madness and divine philosophy, but "better than all wisdom and all human knowledge, because it concentrates within itself the advantages of divinization, the purifying forces of rites carried out, and, in short, all the operations performed when one is possessed by the divine" (*Platonic Theology* I. 25). The word "theurgy," a neologism appearing late in the second century, meant "to make gods" and referred to this practice of assimilation to divinity. Proclus believed the discipline appeared in Plato as well, in particular in the behaviour of the young Socrates in the *Parmenides*. Socrates has just spoken, with some excitement, at great length to Zeno and Parmenides; instead of being annoyed with him, the two philosophers "looked at each other and smiled, as if in admiration of Socrates"; Parmenides, then, prepared to instruct the loquacious neophyte (*Parmenides* 130a). Proclus interprets Socrates's acts — speech at length, stirring up "the divine sparks" — as ritual theurgic preparation.

> And thus Parmenides is moved to address Socrates 'when he had finished.' In this phrase also Plato has given us a divine symbol. When a man is anticipating the appearance of the divine, he must exert himself to stir up the divine spark within him in preparation for participation in higher beings; but when the illumination from above is at hand, he must be silent, and this is what Socrates does. Having roused himself for the reception of these men's insight, having by his own words unfolded and exhibited his fitness for partaking of it, he stops speaking and begins to receive the midwifely instruction that they give him (*Commentary on the Parmenides* II. v. 781).

Socrates's "rousing," for Proclus, is through the theurgic ritual of excessive talk, a prelude to silent illumination. Theurgic practice, then, involved not just ceremonial exercises of physical transformation, but speech and reading as well. Proclus regarded the reading of Plato, the *Parmenides*, the most theological of the dialogues in particular, as a religious act, *religio mentis*; the speech of Socrates, his stirring up, equally was theurgy. Once the suppression of pagan religious images was enforced by Christian authorities later in the fourth century, the manipulation of repositories of divinity, the anagogic ascesis of this, became increasingly linguistic. A ritual, a psychagogic, use of language became the dominant theurgic vehicle in the Academy under the instruction of Proclus, a means of preparing oneself for the reception of higher beings. Such a discipline is an emptying, an uplifting: it is a quickening of proximity.

The word "theourigicos" and its variants appear forty-seven times in the writings of Dionysius; in *The Divine Names*, he speaks of "the statues which are the divine names" (909B), just as Damascius, diadochus, later spoke of "vocal statues," and Proclus himself referred to names as "statues in words," depicting primarily the immaterial Forms (*Commentary on the Parmenides* IV. 851). But how does one ritually "manipulate" language so that its theurgic power is released, hastening the soul to "assimilate itself to a superior being" (Proclus, *Commentary on the Cratylus* 18, 27–19. 17)? This effect is achieved in the Dionysian writings through incantation, liturgy, spiralling iteration, and poetry.

· · ·

Wave after wave of names breaks on the ear of the Dionysian interlocutor; the efficacy of the names is liturgical: they do not replicate reality in speech, but coax one to an at-homeness. Their armature is an apt ontology, but their purpose is not to construct a cosmological understanding in the reader; it is to decentre the ego and to sway one nearer to what one desires; they comprise an inebriative ascesis.

The names, false, partial, misleading, affectively inert if viewed objectively, yet charge-bearing to a subjective construal, fall in gradations. The names are simply praise (652A), shouts, delight: their iterations are phenomenologies, assuring, compelling, shaping contemplative experience: the saying of the names, while descriptions of the reader's interior state, is still meant to establish a final cause for the interlocutor. The pre-eminent name is Good, since "it shows forth all the processions of God" (680B), that is, it shows how these are named by human gratitude, reveals the capacity of the processions to draw individuals from their differentiation toward them. This drawing, says Dionysius, is prayer, which, he is careful to point out, is not a domestication of divine wilderness, but an experience of being pulled that nevertheless offers the illusion of control.

> Imagine a great shining chain hanging downward from the heights of heaven to the world below. We grab hold of it with one hand then another, and we seem to be pulling it down toward us. Actually, it is already there on the heights and down below and instead of pulling it to us we are being lifted upward to that brilliance above, to the dazzling light of those beams (680C).

The chain is the names, their ritual iteration, incantatory, a pulling; the names, identifications of inner states of relief and gratitude only, since divinity itself is beyond appellation, have pneumatic authority: they lift the auditor. The names trace one's response to the divine effects, and they accentuate this response. The manipulation of the chain, the undergoing of the chain, is the ascesis of the complete reprisal of being as a hierarchical beneficence. Imagine, Dionysius invites his fellow presbyter, the Good dwelling "far above the sun, an achetype far superior to its dull image, it sends the rays of its undivided goodness to everything with the capacity...to receive it" (693B). The "rays" of the Good are responsible, for instance, for angelic life—"Their longing for the Good makes them what they are and confers on them their well-being. Shaped by what they yearn for, they exemplify goodness and, as the Law of God requires of them, they share with those below them the good gifts which come their way" (696A). The names, Dionysius's exploratory combing-out of them, foster eros for what they point to, by sketching in such paradigms for desire as angelic life, and this bequeaths identity, giving one a sense of place, this locatedness quickening generosity.

The names are shocks of gratitude for what appears as providence: the author reveals what seems to be these good effects as they manifest themselves, passing through the hierarchy of what is, a plausible, reverent, hymnological cosmogenesis, beginning with angels, passing to souls, to irrational souls, to plants, to lifeless matter. The tracking of each effect, which is an account of each name, is a bespeaking of the cosmos. By spiralling utterance, greater name to lesser name, the lesser yielding to the greater, the fluid machinery, a mobile, providential coherence, in procession, rest and return, is enacted in the planetarium of the reader's mind, and one inches in affect toward what holds the attention; an erotic apokatastasis, an awakening with ultimate political and cosmological significance, begins.

> ...the Good is the cause even for the sources and the frontiers of the heavens, which neither shrink nor expand, and it brought into being the silent...and circular movements of the vast heavens, the fixed orders of starry lights decorating the sky and those special wandering stars, particularly those two rotating sources of light described as "great" by the scriptures, and enabling us to reckon our days and our nights, our months and our years. They set the framework in which time and events are numbered, measured and held together (697B).

The names are also a rehearsal of the erotic dynamism of being, the ecstasy of the going out of divinity and its return: here yet another pattern is established for the imagination. "The Good returns all things to itself and gathers together whatever may be scattered, for it is the divine Source and unifier of the sum total of things. Each being looks to it as source...and as objective" (700A)—inevitably so looks: such a look is the substance of the name "Good," for the

Good is the insensible, unintellectable, unlovable God coming to be experienced as desire in an individual's grateful response to the cosmos, that is, to the ordered beauty of being. The name is the subjective state (645B) — the shock — of gladness for what is. "All things desire it. Everything with a mind and reason seeks to know it, everything sentient yearns to perceive it, everything lacking perception has a living and instinctive longing for it, and everything lifeless and merely existent turns, in its fashion, for a share of it" (700B).

Like poetry, the names possess one sort of veracity while avoiding another. The fluent columns of sound in strong poetry must be true without being objective mimeses — the caprice of wilfully random surrealism dooms the work; an exhaustive photographic equivalency in poetry of, say, domestic life dooms the work. The quality of good poetry, what identifies it as such, is bound up with a truthfulness that is, in part, a telling emotional accuracy in imagery, appearing as a shock of recognition and an ensuing, fleet instruction in what appears to be something one knows yet has not named, an instruction that a strict reason would refuse; this unusual form of veracity, like praise, announces and builds proximity: it lifts and this lifting seems liberation not seduction. The word "light," Dionysius continues, may be applied to the Good; this application shows once more that his treatment of the Good is less cosmology than a phenomenological account of the coming to contemplation that builds from the surprise of gratitude.

The Good is described as the light of the mind, because it illuminates the mind of every supra-celestial being with the light of the mind, and because it drives from souls the ignorance and the error squatting there. It gives them a share of the sacred light (700D).

At first it deals out the light in small amounts and, then, as the wish and longing for more light begin to grow, it gives more and more of itself, shining ever more abundantly on them because they 'loved much' (Luke 7:47) and always it keeps urging them onward and upward as their capacity permits (701A).

The light, *lumen mentis*, has eschatological, political effect, as well, as it "assembles into union everything possessed of reason and mind" (701B). The experience of gratitude, which becomes contemplative focus, further, restores the world's reality: "It returns them toward the truly real...it gathers their clashing fancies into a single, pure, coherent, and true knowledge" (701B), achieving a healing that is both interior and cosmic.

. . .

The holding of the names in the mind, desire's words, expostulations, desire's quickening, the praises that seem appropriate to desire, by which it is formed and sped, is an exercise in uplifting. John Scotus Eriugena, the Latin Church's first translator of the Dionysian writings, renders this interior experience variously in his translation of *The Mystical Theology*, as *sursum agere* (to be driven with violence, to be set in motion upward); *consurgere* (to rise up, to stand up, to rise in honour of someone, to rise in any action, join an insurrection); *elevare* (to be uplifted, raised, to alleviate, to lighten).[4] The inner movement that is the object of Dionysian ascetical theology, then, is violation, courtesy, relief. This is the subjectivity of formation because another name for the Good, says Dionysius, is "beauty." "The sacred writers lift up a hymn of praise to this Good. They call it beautiful, beauty (Song of Songs 1:16, John 4:16, Psalm 45:2), love and beloved." (701C). While this word "beauty" is chiefly response, a light of the mind, it is also obliquely cosmology, emotionally dependable, fecund: what is is known in the jolt of the heart and is read from there—the psalmist, the evangelist "give it [the Good] the names which convey that it is the source of loveliness and the flowering of grace" (701C). Its result is comeliness and symmetry.

The name stands also for the eruption of emotion attendant upon the discovery of oneself being drawn into a community: as "beauty" the Good appears as "the Cause which gathers all into one" (701C).

And there it is ahead of all as Goal, as the Beloved, as the Cause toward which all things move, since it is the longing for beauty which actually brings them into being. It is a mode to which they conform (704A).

The longing hinted at by "beauty" is, says Dionysius, in fact "divine longing...seeking Good for the sake of the Good" (708B). The name is the announcement of the discovery of this eros within the contemplative; its utterance is an ascesis initiating, firming, this discovery. Eriugena's *consurgere* is an encounter with identity—intimate, strange—a falling into oneself, is vivified introspection: it is an alarming, deracinating individuality that is oddly a merging. "This divine yearning brings ecstasy so that the lover belongs not to the self but to the beloved" (712A).

The ecstasy provoked by such language is oxymoronic: the divinity, in erotic passage from itself, remains within itself (712B): the going out, the largesse, the communion, is a stable inwardness. The paradigm makes politics and introspection simultaneous in the contemplative, the Dionysian account of divine eros a provocation of a similar eros. "He is yearning on the move, existent in the Good, flowing out from the Good and into all that is, and returning once again to the Good" (712C–D) in "an everlasting circle" (713D). The double advantage of this image is that it involves a sphere, suggesting the simultaneity of union and multiplicity, and contains the whole of contemplation and erotics in a single thought—such compression, like lyrical economy, astounds and therefore directs as it instructs. For Dionysius, as for

Proclus, language is the primary theurgical instrument: by it
the god is summoned in the one addressed.

· · ·

The succession of numinal approximations, inklings, goes
on. Another name for what is beyond names is "being." This
word, as all of the others, fails to reach what is transcendent,
yet is "a hymn of praise for the being-making procession of
the absolute divine source of being into the total domain of
being"— an expostulatory response, then, to what appears as
providential effulgence. This response hints at an ontology —
such a presumption of ontology is an emotional precondition
of the response — and weds one to such an ontology's dynamism: understanding is a praising and the anagogic work
this hymnic labour does.

In his repeatedly iterated cosmology of the Being-beyond-
being, under its many names, through its multiple effects,
Dionysius insists upon the unknowability of the source of
being, the Pre-existent, while speaking at length of its beneficence. He also insists upon the union of the unsayable and
the sayable.

All the radii of a circle are brought together in the unity of
the centre which contains all the straight lines brought
together within itself. These are linked one to another
because of this single point of origin and they are completely
unified at this centre. As they move a little away from it they

are differentiated a little, and as they fall farther they are farther differentiated (821A).

Yet in every cosmological iteration, the Pre-existent is
exempted —"He is not a facet of being" (824A); "He has every
shape and structure, and yet is formless and beautyless"
(824B). These trackings of the names for procession and the
repeated assertion of the nameless nature of the source are
stagings of the imaginative summoning of positive images of
divinity — the sun; the centre of a circle; the monad holding
every number — and negative ones — formless, beautyless,
nonbeing — and their cancellation, the enactment of apophasis's ascesis. "He is present to all and he is everything...He is
at rest and astir, is neither resting nor stirring...He is in nothing. He is no thing" (825B). Such expressions, incoherent as
ontology, even though they hold the form of ontological
remark, wear away the image, as they retain the attentive
focus the images fashioned. Piety is effaced, to be replaced by
helplessness caught in an erotic undertow.

. . .

Knowing continues to appear as praise in the Dionysian
exploration of the further names —"Wisdom," "Mind,"
"Word," "Truth." "Now, if you will, let us give praise to the
good and eternal Life for being wise, for being the principle
of wisdom, the subsistence of wisdom, for transcending all
wisdom and understanding it" (865B), even as we realize this

Life is unlike "all reason, all intelligence, all wisdom." All human thinking is "a sort of error" (865B) in relation to divine knowing; therefore it is appropriate to apply negative terms to God, though not in the sense of deprivation. One version of negation is oddness in utterance, "dissimilar similarity." The divinity, however, is not approached by the absurd, the strange (865C) — speech of, say, the "foolishness" of God (1 Cor. 1:25) — but such symbolism possesses transformative power: its impropriety blocks discursive reason, yet apt strangeness still pulls the knower to what would be known: it drives upward with violence in the Eriugenean sense of *sursum agere*.

The intent of the Dionysian interpretive process, tending ultimately toward negation, is ecstasy by which we are "taken out of ourselves and become wholly of God" (868A), who is unintellectable, indeed unreachable by all appetite. The end of noesis is such high-pitched noetic disappointment. Belonging to God rather than ourselves, in this disorientation, this homelessness, "the divine gifts [will] be poured out onto us" (868A). This cognitive uprooting, the result of praise gathering into negation, the result of strange praise, is a form of similitude, for "Wisdom" has neither reason nor intelligence itself, is not, that is, bordered by the limits of either power, even while it is the source of both.

> God is therefore known in all things and as distinct from all things. He is known through knowledge and unknowing. Of him there is conception, reason, understanding, touch, per-

ception, opinion, imagination, name, and many other things. On the other hand, he cannot be understood, words cannot contain him, and no name can lay hold of him (872A).

The divinity, "known" through the assertions of kataphasis and the withdrawls of apophasis, is intimacy that is built by the full repetitions of kataphatic cosmology, which are reading's theurgy, and the names's apophatic delimitation. The knowledge of apophasis, higher, holds no content, is a sort of dying, a seeming madness (873A). But even with negation, though this language is truer, one does not leave the subjectivity of the conceptual, as Proclus sharply reminds readers in his remarks on the *Parmenides*: such cancellations "do not express anything about the One, but do refer to the One."

> For nothing at all applies to it, either specifically or privately, but, as we have said, the name 'one' names our conception of it, not the One itself, and so we say that their negation also is about conception, and none of the negative conclusions that have been stated is about the One, but because of its simplicity, it is exalted above all contrast and all negation (*Comm. on the Parmenides* VII. 70K).

When even the negations of assertion about divinity must be themselves negated, since even they represent conceptual limitations and present misdirecting cognitive consolations, it is clear that understanding in this erotic noesis is entirely formational.

Just as there deliberation ought to be eliminated from our activity, although it is brought to perfection by deliberation, so here all dialectical activity ought to be eliminated. These dialectical operations are the preparation for the strain toward the One, but are not themselves the strain. Or rather, not only must it be eliminated, but the strain as well. Finally, when it has completed its course, the soul may rightly abide with the One. Having become single and alone in itself, it will choose only the simply One (*Comm. on the Parmenides* VII. 74K).

Learning ending in wisdom is formation through which aroused interiority is brought to act with such apparent volitional inevitability.

. . .

Liturgy, too, for Dionysius, is a place of theurgic alteration. Here, as well, knowing is undergone, but, as with the psychagogery of reading, this operation does not require the reader to grasp anything with the understanding (*mathein*), as Aristotle says of the knowledge of initiates, but "to have a certain inner experience (*pathein*) and so to be put in a particular frame of mind, presuming that they are capable of this frame of mind in the first place."[5] Such is the experience of theurgy, which for Proclus was "a power higher than all human wisdom"; such, too, is the *anagogia* of "idle talk" that Socrates enjoins in particular upon the young in the *Parmenides*—the uselessness of dialectic and not "mere argumentation and logical procedures" which the multitude admire—that Proclus calls "a force that leads the soul upwards to the truth" (*Comm. on the Parmenides* v. 990).

Liturgy is knowing that occurs in the ritual activity of the community, "the perfect total of all its sacred constituents," as Dionysius says in *The Ecclesiastical Hierarchy* (373C), a sociable noesis taking the forms of purification, illumination, and perfection. It is enacted by a triad of ministers—deacons, priests, hierarchs—and received by a triad of beneficiaries— those outside of initiation (catechumens) or who have become disjoined from initiation (penitents); the laity; and monks. The ecclesiastically authorized order of service echoes the providentialism of the cosmos, where "the being and proportion and order" in each member of the hierarchy is deified, "then imparted to those below him" (*The Ecclesiastical Hierarchy* 372D). Thus "each one is able to have as great as possible a share in him who is truly beautiful, wise, and good" (373A); this sharing is a rising: where the *anagogia* of *The Divine Names* was conceptual, it is symbolic—choreographic—in *The Ecclesiastical Hierarchy*. This sharing itself is knowledge, is deification (376D), "using images derived from the senses," a plastic, not linguistic, theurgy.

Knowing as ritual abolishes the usual distance of the knower: one approaches what one would know, comes to conformability not comprehension, to "likeness" and "union" by "sacred enactment" (392A). The first of these illuminating movements is baptism's initiatory submission; before an

intermediary, one promises "complete obedience to whatever is laid upon him" (393B). Eros brings one first to nothing,
within which alacrity appears: the candidate eager for baptism approaches with "fright and uncertainty" (393B). This
sacred enactment of approach provokes a responsive gesture
in the putative teacher who prostrates himself within the
liturgy before the sign of the divine eros in the appetite of
the one called; the "uplifting" of the catechumen begins
with marks of the experience of nothingness—he is "naked
and barefoot" in the ceremony—being brought into the
sacred community, for this knowing he seeks steps from a
stripping and requires "the mediation of people more
advanced than he" (400C). But these baptismal enactments
do not amount to an "inspired existence"; they do, however,
begin an "incubation" within the "paternal scriptures" (432D),
an immurement in reading.

The deacons, whose charism is purification, constrain
the catechumens to absent themselves before the synaxis,
the Eucharistic gathering, the communitarian noesis par
excellence, which fashions personal and, ultimately, ontological unity: "Every sacredly initiating operation draws our
fragmented lives together in one-like divinization" (424C):
the synaxis achieves this more efficiently than any other
psychagogic instrument. It is preceded by a sung creed, a
"symbol of adoration," a hierarchic thanksgiving, a celebration of the totality of divine theurgy, by which one receives a
share of "the divine condition and uplifting" (436C–D). The
creed is a manipulation of the "statue" of a memory longer

than but inclusive of one's own (441C). While the symbols of scripture are protected from anarchic curiosity by difficulty, the symbols of numinal action are hidden within *disciplini arcani* — the discipline of secrecy, thus saved from reductive dissipation into scholastic sifting, saved from misconstrual. Yet their work of God is achieved in their being performed; their theurgical power also is released by Dionysius's description of them; their theurgy is achieved in the imagination of the presbyter who reads these descriptive accounts of ritual.

. . .

The Hellenic religious world was in decline at the end of the fourth century. Sculptural representations of the gods were proscribed in the Empire in 386; the orator Libranius described to the Emperor Theodosius the spectacle of "torrents" of Christian monks moving through the countryside, destroying all temples they came upon; the effect was as if, he said, they were tearing the eye out of a region[6]; villagers, Libranius reported, lost their will to work once these traditional links with the gods appeared to have been severed; starvation seemed a possibility. The Hellenist poet C. P. Cavafy, in poems such as "Priest at Serapeion" and "Kleitos's Illness," captures some of the disorientation of this time. But according to the Syrian Iamblichus, the dominant Platonist philosopher of the age, the enervation endured by the traditional religion was not the result of Christian proselytization, but "the endless innovations and lawlessness of the Hellenes" (*De*

Mysteriis VII. 5). He echoes here Plato's denunciation of spiritual and ritual invention in the *Laws* (*Laws* 657a). Iamblichus
bemoaned in particular the extreme rationalism of contemporary Platonism, contrasting its hybris with the stability of
the Egyptians in hieratic matters (*DM* VII. 5).

Iamblichus's probing of the Egyptian mysteries, *De
Mysteriis*, was an attempt to bring the foundational, subterranean element of Plato, which Plato himself insisted he had
imported from Egypt (*Statesman* 290c–e, *Timaeus* 21, *Phaedrus*
275b, *Laws* 819b, *Philebus* 18b, *Charmides* 156b–157c), into prominence. In Plotinus, the soul did not descend into being;
indeed nature appears in the *Enneads* as a source of temptation (*Enneads* IV. 4. 43. 23–6). Plotinus complains, as well, in
this passage, about magic, a particularly vicious form of
externality. For Plato, however, and for Iamblichus, the cosmos was a crucial part of philosophical healing: the lost
harmony of a polis returned when "its sacrifices and
feasts...fit the true nature order" (*Laws* 809e); further, Plato
argued, when ritual is responsive to the cosmos, the intelligence of humans is increased (*Laws* 809e): to be drawn into
the gods, one needed to act in concert with the revelation of
divinity in the natural order. The therapy of paideia, thus,
drew one from self-assertion to such concert; theurgy, a
physical, acted-out knowing suited to the soul's embodied
state, was its most potent tool.[7]

The Father of the Universe, in the *Timaeus*, created
humans by mixing in the same bowl in which he combined
all the original elements of the universe, divine and material,

"what was left of the former ingredients" (*Timaeus* 41e); human souls, "the lowest of the divine beings" (*De Mysteriis* I. 10) were, thus, a composite of everything. While no detailed record of theurgic ceremonies exists, it is known that they involved the ritual use of stones, plants, and animals: because such objects were particularly intimate to human beings, humans having been formed from different allotments of the same substances, and because these objects bore the "signatures" of the gods, they possessed a peculiar power to provoke a recollection of origin and the reformation of a life.

> ...for since it was proper not even for terrestrial things to be utterly deprived of participation in the divine, earth also has received from it a share in divinity such as is sufficient for it to be able to receive the gods. Observing this, and discovering in general, in accordance with the properties of each of the gods, the receptacles adapted to them, the theurgic art in many cases links together stones, plants, animals, aromatic substances, and other such things that are sacred, perfect and godlike, and then from all these composes an integrated and pure receptacle (*DM* v. 23).

Rods, pieces of wood, pebbles, stones, corn, or wheat (*DM* III. 17), though soulless, manifest the gods, make "all things clear and known," though they themselves have no knowledge. But they must be disturbed from their usual setting by insertion in ritual for their capacity to draw understanding to be released; the dawning of this understanding has nothing to do with human intellectual endeavour: theurgy, indeed, "reveals thoughts that surpass all knowledge" (DM III. 17). Rhythms and melodies; particular movements; certain forms of speech bore the signature, the "sunthemata," of the gods; the marks of divinity in incantation, certain names, designs scratched on the ground, exposed in ceremony, equally could pull interiorities outside of thinking into divinity. Human embodiment, the soul's ontic familiarity with things, meant that its most promising approach to divinity was necessarily epistemologically unlit, an oblique way of unknowing.

In the ascesis of ritual, one did what one could not know, the form of one's action assuming the form of divine creative action, the providentialism of cosmogenesis; this congruence, however, was not an object for self-awareness: theurgy was efficacious while remaining ineffable. Indeed, the "meaninglessness" of symbols, the chanted names of the gods for instance, was central to their anagogic power: "And indeed, if [the name] is unknowable to us, this very fact is its most sacred aspect, for it is too excellent to be divided into knowledge."(DM VII. 4). The indivisible names, unfriable because of their incoherence, matched "the mystical and ineffable image of the Gods " in the soul, and these monadic names, iterated, chanted, held whole in the puzzled voice, woke the soul (DM VII. 4). Unlike the soteriology of Plotinus and Porphyry, Iamblichus's path of renewal included a form of prayer; the affective source of this prayer was poverty (DM I. 15) that would not turn from the cognitive emptiness of "tokens" of divinity, but would find its appetite, imageless, starved of presumption, build before it.

. . .

The presbyter's work is to draw the imagination of initiates into the beneficence and compassion of the artifact of divine eros, being itself, provident, shapely, where what is higher attends to what is lower, where all things operate as paradigms of obedience to others; thus those instructed may return to what is estranged in themselves. The presbyters, "light-bearing," (*EH* 505D) achieve this charismatic healing, "initiating others into the hierarchy," (505A) through rites "which are images of the power of divinity"(505B): theirs is the theurgic gift of bestirring the erotics of memory aside from thinking, the instigation of home-going through "divine working," in those who have been purged by a diaconate, so that they are made "receptive to the ritual vision and communion" (508A), incubated within "cleansing enlightenments" (509B) and the enclaustration of scripture.

The theurgic formation enacted through the presbyter, Dionysius suggests, begins with the ceremonial movements of those involved in his consecration (509B–516C): even the fact that the priest kneels on both knees in the ordination ceremony, while the deacon kneels on one during his initiation, has anagogic import: the cleric's humility is shown as double, as his charism is — he purifies, he uplifts — and his enactment of this sign works this quality into him, as it forms the attentiveness of those to be uplifted, preparing them "to enter contemplation"(516B). All are enfolded, thus, through the symbolism in ceremony, into the erotic dynamism of the cosmic hierarchy as they act it out in ritual, the hierarch who "receives on his head the scriptures," laying hands on the presbyter, the presbyter acting out his doubly bent state under the "divine yokes" (516B), the purged lifted — and so a restoration of a luminous polis in transformative gesture is made to appear.

. . .

The apotheosis of the *corpus dionysiacum*, *The Mystical Theology*, that poem exercising such great influence on the theology of the Western church, that small, succinct medicine, is yet another linguistic ritual performed for the presbyter Timothy; its therapeutic purpose — correction and illumination — again matches the sort of receptivity native to the charism of the priest. It includes, as do *The Divine Names* and *The Ecclesiastical Hierarchy*, a sketch of the beginning of the universe, an account negated even as it is uttered: the poem is a formational exercise appearing as mimesis then cancelled as representation, a linguistic healing as an incantatory uplifting.

Trinity!! Higher than any being,
    any divinity, any goodness!
  Guide of Christians
    in the wisdom of heaven!

Lead us beyond unknowing and light,
    up to the farthest, highest peak
                of mystic scripture,
    where the mysteries of God's Word
      lie simple, absolute and unchangeable
      in the brilliant darkness of a hidden silence.
Amid the deepest shadow
    they pour overwhelming light
    on what is most manifest.
Amid the wholly unsensed and unseen
    they completely fill our sightless minds
    with treasures beyond all beauty.

                                  (MT 997A–B)

This introductory language presents a spiritual exercise to the reader, in which the imagination is induced again to hold the complete architecture of the cosmos, the manifest world, and the logos hidden (*mystikos*) above or within it; once the imagination is so contorted, attentive in such an impossible way, it is enjoined to undo itself—"leave behind you everything perceived and understood, everything perceptible and understandable, all that is not and all that is, and, with your understanding laid aside, to strive upward as much as you can…"(997B). The interior eye, under these counter pressures, is "undivided" and abandoned, enduring anagogy in this transfixed emptiness, "uplifted to the ray of the divine shadow," a dazzling darkness (1000A). The formational endeavour is augmented by secrecy ("see to it that none of this comes to the hearing of the unformed" (1000A)). The unformed are those overtaken by the powers of discursive thought, by dogmatic theology, by the bright surface of the physical world in such a way that being cannot become an object of contemplation—such preoccupations place initiation into divinity beyond reach. To disclose the true nature of things in the context of such noetic commitments would shut down all aspects of theurgic initiative. Some sort of collapse of such powers indeed is a precondition for philosophic speech, for the Cause that is both "eloquent and taciturn" is manifest only "to those who travel through foul and fair, who pass beyond the summit of every ascent, who leave behind them every divine light, every voice, every word from heaven, and who plunge into the darkness..." (1000C). In such a cognitive stripping, knowing is a being-taken-in, a "belonging" where one is "neither oneself nor someone else" (1001A).

The approach to this knowing is not a prehension but a "clearing aside" (*aphaeresis*) of, among other things, understandings set in place by the exhaustive praises of affirmative theology; but this cancelling is not anti-rationalist obscurantism: it is the height of reason. This knowing involves no stretch to an object but a trued subjectivity; it is more than ineffable, an active unknowing (1033B). This unknowing itself, still, is more than the negation of assertion in the *via positiva*: what the contemplative "belongs" to is equally beyond denial; it is not conceptual; it is not power; it is not light, not wisdom, not divinity, not goodness, not being, not nonbeing (1048A–D), yet it permits, or rather is, consanguinity.

Five
....

THE WORK OF DESIRE

THE *Cloud of Unknowing*, convivial, confiding, anonymous, fourteenth century, traces the life of those stirred. Do not read this book, the author warns, unless you have begun the practice it describes—if you do not already know intimately what the book says, have not striven, that is, "long time before" to come to a contemplative living (1),[1] are not gusted now by an "inward stirring under the privy counsel of God," while still not knowing what you do (2), readership only will place you at risk. "Whisperers, tale-bearers," the curious learned in particular must not meddle with this book; even those practised in the active life of good works should spend no time with it. The proscription is an act of mercy: the book inevitably will appear to the nonerotic as something it is not—as technique, as analysis, as dogma on the mystical life, as a yardstick of piety. Not only will it not cohere as any of these—will require an impossible subsidizing energy; it will be lost to caricature—but it will manufacture error (2): it will place in the unengaged reader one of a variety of interior difficulties that the book will be powerless to undo. The book, then, cannot be read safely from a distance; readership, in its case, involves a particular labour. This position is not self-selecting, nor is the labour shaped by one's purpose: the erotic ambition of the book's true reader places certain necessary tasks before him and with these the book will act as a balm. *The Cloud of Unknowing* cannot be instruction, in other words, only confirmation within such a life, can be nothing other than comfort. And it can succour, of course, only those who have entered the undertaking—perhaps without choosing this, perhaps without knowing what they do—it has under consideration. It works in this way as a tessera of phenomenology, idiosyncratic, yet useful to others; it can tell you where you are or might have been in a journey well under way. It is closed to those who have not started; it is a therapy that imperils those not caught in the desire it tracks.

· · ·

The book stands in a rich tradition of ascetical and mystical theology—Augustine, pseudo-Dionysius the Areopagite, John Scotus Eriugena, Bernard of Clairvaux—but its premier authority is Richard of St. Victor, prior of the abbey of St. Victor, especially his work on ascesis *The Twelve Patriarchs* or *Benjamin Minor*, and his treatise on contemplation, *The Mystical Ark* or *Benjamin Major*, works written between 1153 and 1162. *The*

Twelve Patriarchs is a tropological reading of Genesis 25: 19–35, the tale of Jacob, "a quiet man living in tents" (Gen. 25:27), his wives, Leah and Rachel, his twelve sons and one daughter. Richard grasps these characters as the pattern of an interior life that ends in contemplative attention; this life arrives at its apogee with the birth of the youngest child, Benjamin, "a young man in ecstasy of mind," figure for the highest forms of contemplation. But it begins with the birth of Ruben, Leah's first son, whose name means "God has seen my abasement," and who represents the vision of God through an "intuition of dread" (*The Twelve Patriarchs* VIII).

The text of scripture, for Richard, possesses, unlike virtually all other books, an instructive, transformative hiddenness; it is "written on the inside of the page and the outside," (Rev. 5:1, Ezek. 2:10) able to satisfy those with a mystical appetite, while providing "pasture" to those content with what shows clearly.[2] The interior writing is not an argument, not a proof, not system, not dogma, but a psychagogic shape holding the power to place a turn in the psyche of particular readers. Let the mind play on this shimmering hiddenness, on this recessed, supraluminous writing, sequestered, lost almost without trace in the story, and it will begin to enact the occult pattern it apprehends.

The two mothers, Leah and Rachel, monitor the rising of the soul: Leah, fruitful but with poor eyesight, represents affection; Rachel, more beautiful but nearly sterile, stands for reason. Leah is drawn by the pull of divine inspiration; Rachel is caught in the flame of divine showing (*The Twelve*

Patriarchs, IV). Jacob, while seeking Rachel, unexpectedly finds himself in the embrace of Leah, Laban's eldest daughter, sent to Jacob's tent on his marriage night (Gen. 29:23–35): the route to contemplation passes through the ordering of the affections, this a jarring, a revulsion to the besotted, long-serving knower. Leah's weak vision means she loves with inevitable imprudence, eros endlessly attaching itself to what are distractions. The correction of this misalignment of desire, manifesting itself in prayer as psychic garrulity, drunken-ness, begins with an experience of affliction (Gen. 29:32), a "holy fear," Ruben's birth, and proceeds through a series of shocks — grief, hatred of what one is, and so on — ending in the appearance of "ordered shamefacedness," represented by the birth of Jacob's solitary daughter, Dina ("that judge-ment"). Richard's ascesis is not the work of an angelistic will, but builds, he says, from an "inner sweetness," an "ecstasy of mind" (*The Twelve Patriarchs* XXXIV; XL); one is drawn to it by a brush with quintessential beauty: the fruit of contempla-tion unaccountably precedes the undertaking of it, shame growing from ecstatic sweetness. One must begin the prac-tice before he enters the contemplative life, a decisionless beginning, the brief achievement of the end coming before and shaping the seeking of it. The full enjoyment of contem-plation, in Richard's schema, however, follows shame: Benjamin is born after Dina. His mother dies at his birth (Gen. 35:18): reason has no place in the experience of con-templative seeing, though it is indispensable in the approach to it.

. . .

The Cloud of Unknowing is addressed to a twenty-four-year-old cleric who has recently begun to live as a solitary, perhaps a Carthusian. The book is meant to aid him in the task of introspection he has already begun, the "busy beholding to the course and the manner" of his calling; the matter under examination is desire, for his calling, *The Cloud* makes clear, is an erotic one in which he is led by "a leash of a lovely longing" (3). His chief work now is to "all ways stand in desire" (5) throughout his life: this work is a continuation and a spreading of his present practice. The desire that directs his life appears somewhat estranged from him: he stands in it, while it appears to stand outside him and pull him; his work, he is told, is merely to "consent" to it (5), undergo it. Though pulled, however, he still requires direction (4): part of this direction is aid offered in the uncovering of a pattern in all longing.

The intent life, the life that is stirred, *The Cloud* says, has a watercourse: the Common, Special, Singular, and Perfect lives: the first three — the ordinary lay life, the clerical life, the solitary life — can be begun and finished within nature and within the span of one's natural life; the last can be begun now but comes to term only in *beatitudo*. A "boisterous beholding" gives *The Cloud* author the stages of this progression — the highest insight in this phenomenology, this direction, can be nothing more than an eyeballing in; he undermines his observations as science — yet each are inevitable, given desire: "in the same order and in the same course" do they come (3): one's wanting in this work is fastened to this ghostly pulling; one is tugged along: you feel, then, the draw in your wanting that completes the erotic teleology, yet do not experience it as teleology. The desirer simply acquiesces; his desire shapes his will until in all his life he stands in desire, and this desire flows to a single point: all one does in the life of contemplation is look at divinity and let it act as it pleases (5). In this state of transfixity, you move toward pliancy; you move toward loneliness, in which you turn away from creatures and their works with apparent carelessness; this turning away is "the work of the soul that most pleaseth God" (5), and is oddly altruistic, "cleansing," and brings to virtue not only the one detached but strangers as well. None of this can be accomplished by the will—it is a hard and wonderful thing to do with that muscle (6)—but is extremely easy, "the lightest work of all," when the soul is visited by, as Richard Methley has it in his fifteenth-century Latin translation, *sensibili delectatione*, a sensible pleasure or lust.

> Lift up thine heart unto God with a meek stirring of love; and mean himself and none of his goods. And thereto look that thou loathe to think on aught but himself so that nought work in thy mind nor in thy will but only himself. And do all that is in thee is to forget all the creatures that ever God made and the works of them, so that thy thought or thy desire be not directed or stretched to any of them, neither in general nor in special. But let them be with a seemly recklessness, and take no heed of them (5).

Such a focus—the life of looking and passivity, a leaving of others and what they do, these things subsequently contracting into autonomy (7)—produces an experience of profound disorientation in the one so drawn, an interior darkness that the book calls the cloud of unknowing, a stretch of epistemic crisis, which leaves only an arrested desire—a naked intent unto God—that seems to bear no relation to human purpose. It, in fact, appears initially to stand over and above such purpose, subverting, rearranging. The soul wants nothing other than divinity, but it experiences this now as distance, something unavailable to interior sight, to reason, to affect: all these powers are disabled by the dark. One is denuded of what identity these bring; one is cast outside one's life, placed in unlikeness, an unconsoled state in which even the hope of divine proximity is removed (10–11).

The temptation to console oneself will be strong under these circumstances. One may seek, for instance, the "profit" of "minding" others, ghostly or made, in this state of deprival, "minding" the qualities of God, the charm of the saints, the delight of heaven—may wish to undergo the ordinary images of conventional religious life: but these ministrations, proferred by the imagination, their piety notwithstanding, in fact debilitate and must be eschewed, even though such meditations appear to feed contemplative purpose. In fact they muddle the aim of the one in contemplation, "the eye of a shooter...upon the prick that he shooteth to" (11), enervate this evacuated look by draping its nakedness with forms and must be hid, says the author, in a cloud of forgetting, in favour of an affective life above the imagination, above thinking, a life of "smiting" that thick cloud with "a sharp dart of longing love" (12).

．　．　．

The apophaticism of *The Cloud* draws on Richard of St. Victor's contemplative epistemology traced in *The Twelve Patriarchs* and *The Mystical Ark*. In the last book, a treatise on the forms of mystical prayer, Richard gives six levels of contemplation: in imagination and according to imagination; in imagination and according to reason; in reason and according to imagination; in reason and according to reason; above but not beyond reason; above and seemingly beyond or against reason (*The Mystical Ark* Bk. I, VI). Each of these stages, which may be roughly simultaneous as well as sequential, is an attempt to surmount the near-impossibility of the "carnal mind" rising to the knowledge of "invisible things" (*The Twelve Patriarchs* XIV); in this effort, the imagination, rendering impalpabilities into visible forms, is the most primitive faculty, yet a necessary propaedeutic to higher forms of attention, bringing reason to "that place to which it did not know how to go by means of itself" (*The Mystical Ark* Bk. II, XVII). The imagination, mobile, lifting the mind to wherever "wonder carries it" (*The Mystical Ark* Bk. I, VI), breeds amazement, preparing reason for the task for which it must sublate itself to complete in the growing contemplative, drawing reason to its limit; but the imagination has no competence with that sweep of phenomena for which visible similitudes would be reductive: it is neither probing nor prudent here, but rather Phaedrusean in the range of its delight, indiscriminate, conflating unlike things that have but a surface resemblance. In the sixth "watchtower of contemplation," reason itself is subverted in preference for a permeability permitting the "irradiation of divine light," an alert, craning passivity, the early formation of which is the achievement of the imagination, breeding in the mind an alacrity for ravishment. An effort to visualize the Trinity, say, one of the numinous things beyond both imagination and reason, or to offer a plausible account of it, forecloses on the possibility of its contemplation. This observation is not an obscurantist norm but a remark on an epistemological economy. *The Cloud* writer, avid, with hybristic appetite for what is higher, elects to "leave all that thing that I can think, and choose to love that thing I cannot think" (12). This work is not arduous, given erotic engagement, or long: "the shortest work of all that man may imagine. It is neither longer nor shorter than an atom..." (6), equal, exactly, to a single volitional stirring.

· · ·

Erudition is a danger; curiosity is a danger; "natural wit" is a danger: yet *The Cloud* does not press for a naïve intuitionism; it is not anti-intellectual, not Romantic, not interested in the promotion of religious vitalism. It does resist, though, the hegemony of reason: this power is not equal to all tasks, though it is prone to a misleading solicitude in which it conceives it is. God is incomprehensible to knowing, but not to loving, where he appears as "sweetness" (8), the feel of the cognition of paradise.

The contemplative must set himself against "thoughts": these enervate the naked gaze; efforts to explain the nature of the look are emigrations from contemplative practice. "And if any thought rise and will press all ways above thee, betwixt thee and that darkness, and ask thee saying: 'What seekest thou, and what wouldst thou have?' say thou, 'that it is God that thou wouldst have...' And in him, say, 'thou has no skill.' And therefore say 'Go thou down again'; and tread him fast down again with a stirring of love, although he seem to thee right holy, and seem to thee as if he would help thee to seek him" (12).

The force of analytic inquiry, outside the sphere of its competence, is a kind of dissipation: it decays into "chatter"; the pursuit of questions it fosters becomes a "scattering"; the interior representation of noumenal things one seeks turns into a lowering; the ratiocinative impulse must be "trod down" in this cloud of forgetting. This sort of probe, enthusiastic to depict all moments of intentionality, which the book bars from the higher forms of attention, is nevertheless necessary in the lower ranges: indeed, these are the very efforts that make the later suprarational forms of contemplation possible; they assemble the proper telos for such attention and wed the mind to it; in a sense, they should never be jettisoned, though in the further reaches of contemplation must be kept in utter quietude in the cloud of forgetting. The ghost of these efforts remains in the fixity and the trueness of the contemplative gaze: yet if these same efforts were to turn toward the focus they had assembled, they would leave it "broken" and "undone" (14). The cloud of forgetting is a refusal of reason its consolations once it strays beyond its gift.

The ambition for "a sharp and clear beholding" (15), present in all forms of discursive thinking, is nature, is good: inquiry in pursuit of explanation brings the unlike toward the human sphere by finding it a home in human language and taxonomy; it locates the individual in the scheme of things, and thus is the rudiment of humility. Reason's highest work undertaken in the lower part of contemplative life is, then, ascetical: the placing of the human in the largest of all possible accounts, quickening "good ghostly meditations and busy beholdings unto a man's own wretchedness with sorrow and contrition" (16), these exercises, as mathematics for the Pythagoreans, training the mind to awe. Reason is wrongly employed, *The Cloud* author says, when it supposes it alone can accomplish what the contemplative finally seeks —"to be knit to God in spirit, in onehead of love and accordance of will" (16) —when in fact all it can manage is a oneness in human terms, a reduction of unspeakability to speech; here a self-flattering caricature appears. The true union cannot be achieved in nature, only in grace: a phantom limb of interior seeking, thus, lies above the rational probe: an emptiness, a lack, an availability is higher, though to be genuine it must be an artifact of reason manifest as discernment. A confused, unsatisfied, blind stirring of wanting is better than an apparently clear beholding of even the highest things: this burnished clarity simply blocks the reached-for darkness.

This blind stirring is not a search for knowledge, but a reformation of the one who experiences it: it finds no clarity, unearths no account of what it cranes toward, yet only the stability, the singleness of mind native to this naked intent can bestir virtue, the form of ekstasis, for Plotinus, in everyday life, in particular the encompassing virtues of humility and charity. Humility has a special noumenal efficiency here, for in its perfect form — the dumbfounding that comes from awe before what is divine — it provokes a faultless ordering of the affections (24). One cannot visualize or name the divine but can become what participates in what divinity is — without, of course, having a firm sense that this is what one does — taking on the mum noesis of identity: this is a return to one's first state, a going home. Out of this inchoate, non-reportable, helpless transfixity before the dark cloud of what one cannot say comes an approach to prelapsarian health, for this erotic reaching alone "destroyeth the ground and the root of sin" (21).

This is a hidden labour: it appears to be preoccupation with nothing to those who stand outside it and inevitably arouses their disapproval (29) — Martha's protest over Mary's alert attention (Luke 10:38–42), says *The Cloud*, is the paradigmatic instance of such an evaluation — since to the noncontemplative, grounds for the strenuous engagement do not appear to exist; it itself appears to be a wasting of

time. Awestruck humility carves down the contemplative — it carves only the one who has fallen into the gaze:
ravishment quells one to a sweet gravitas. One so hushed
will not mount a defence in the face of the disapproval of the
nonerotic: to do so would be to slide from the gaze, and the
wish for this would not occur to one held in transfixity. One
in this work, further, seeks no release from pain, no increase
of reward, nought but the gaze, the heart's ocularity. The
contemplative "hath no leisure" to distinguish among persons, preferring one to the other (37): all are equally dear (38);
he has no interest other than this beating on the cloud: nothing beneath this comforts (34). Humility is a "forgetting" of
what lies beneath this blind stirring, an uninterest in consolation other than the qualified, subverted, virtually erased
consolation of contemplation; it is the end of amour-propre,
the ground of wanting lesser things; it is the not-feeling of
one's entitlement. An avidity for the one thing necessary
(Luke 10:42) breeds detachment elsewhere: humility grows
from ravishment, and is the simplification and intensification of desire.

. . .

The life of contemplation begins with shame — is preceded
by the birth of Dina: at its furthest reach, it is a self-forgetting
that is simultaneous with attention to divine things that are
above and seemingly beyond reason (The Mystical Ark Bk. IV,
IX), the embarrassment of reason that would be impossible

without the exercise of reason. But the contemplative life precedes the extrarational experience of contemplation in the form of a particular fixity of mind: "And loathe to think on aught under God. And go not thence for anything that befalleth" (21). This transfixity of mind, this "blind stirring of love," has a transformative power that exceeds that of even the most extreme ascetical practices (21): desire alone in *The Cloud of Unknowing* alters the one who would know.

The representation of anything, but especially pious things, simply deflects this desire: theological rumination, ontological curiosity, disarm the ascetical transformative power within erotic engagement. The probing thought, bent on the transmutation of divinity into image, into speech, keen to provoke virtue "will let thee see the wonderful kindness of God, and if thou listen to him, he desireth not better. For soon after, he will let thee see thine old wretched living; and, peradventure, in seeing and thinking thereof, he will bring to thy mind some place that thou hast dwelt in before this time. So that, at last, ere ever thou knowest, thou shalt be scattered, thou knowest not where. This cause of this scattering is: that first thou didst wilfully listen to that thought, and then thou didst answer him, receive him, and let him have his way" (13). Here the ascesis of eros, noetically sightless, is the higher form of knowing, reaching beyond both the imagination and reason, opposed to them in their protean, invasive state, even though it is formed by the energy of both (13). It is not a knowing, but an altering to a shape that is a version, an ideogram, of what cannot be said.

If there is to be any speech associated with the higher form of prayer, the naked intent "lapped and folden in one word, so that thou mayest have better hold thereupon," *The Cloud* author insists it should be no more than monosyllabic expostulation. This is the "short and pure" prayer of St. Benedict (*Rule of St. Benedict* 20), the versicle of John Cassian (Ps. 69:2) that does not distract desire but moulds it, intensifies it; it is a vehicle of forgetting, driving down sequential thought, repelling the lushness of imagination (13–4; *Conf.* 10. 10); it is a means "to beat on this cloud and this darkness above thee" (14).

The "cloud of unknowing" itself is a cognitive incapacity that has an ascetical effect: a stripping preparatory to deference: beat ever more on this cloud. Such a pressing brings one to meekness and charity (22), the dispositions that encapsulate all virtue. The desire to know, without the hope of comprehension, the disoriented, epektatic eros of contemplation, smooths and arranges the affections into the harmony of virtue (22; *The Mystical Ark* Bk. IV, IX).

· · ·

One beats on the cloud with a naked intent; this nakedness is threefold: one's desire is without image, without anticipation, without consolation. You pursue no lifting of discomfort; the "perfect prentice" "recketh nor regardeth whether he is in pain or in bliss" (36), but is housed in an empty wanting. The emptiness of the reach has two sources: the blinding, disarming impulse of desire and the hard work of forgetting.

The practice of this momentumed, alacritous emptiness is initially taxing but becomes light-filled and restful as devotion builds (39).

Sometimes the cloud is penetrated from above by the dusky illumination of nonreportable, nonrepresentable contemplative insight, which explains little, which may be spoken only with the great peril of misspeaking it and alienating oneself from its power, yet which, like affect-heavy metaphor when undergone but not comprehended, intensifies emotion, heightening one's proximity to the beloved, while abolishing the distance of knowing.

> Then will he sometimes peradventure send out a beam of ghostly light, piercing this *cloud of unknowing* that is betwixt thee and him, and show thee some of his secrets, the which man may not and cannot speak. Then shalt thou feel thine affection inflamed with the fire of his love, far more than I can tell, or may or will at this time (39).

The tongue cannot speak such incidents well, threatens inevitably to transform them to hurt.

. . .

The work of contemplation—the travail of forgetting, the easy labour of blind beating against what cannot come to speech, the stirring, the quick visitations—demands a separation from the place of reward, of redress, of efforts to seek release from pain, of the enjoyment of consolation, of plotting its increase; it works such a separation. Equally, it requires a removal from the active life, the altruistic political world of service, where the common good is sought (40). Both this life and the life of the world and the consolations of each are sublated by the contemplative undertaking, a psycho-ontological political work, a work of repair, restoring the well-being "where all woe is wanting," lost through the erotic deformity of Adamic sin (41). It is an apparently apolitical undertaking rejuvenating politics. The restoration it manages reinstitutes the interior balance of ordered affections, the "cleanness" of awe and wanting before what is divine, an accord within creation. The life of desire anticipates the beauty of Doomsday (41).

The more the nakedness — the emptiness — of erotic pressing is compromised by the consolations of visualizations, however, of images of location and anticipation, by representations of satisfaction ("stirrings of sin"), the more the momentum of this beating decays, and the contemplative work of apokatastasis is jeopardized: it can be lost entirely to its slyest counterfeit, the peopled, fully-rendered religious imagination; with this, one is exiled from the eros of contemplation. *The Cloud* recommends two interior exercises for relief from the weight of thoughts: pretend that they do not press with such force, while looking over their shoulder at what they obscure, the divinity enclefted in unknowability; if this fails, "cower then down under them as a caitlif and a coward overcome in battle; and think that it is but folly to strive any longer with them; and therefore thou yieldest thyself to God in the hands of thine enemies," willing an engulfment, identifying oneself with helplessness: this will tip into a love-sense of liquefaction (Ps. 21:15; *The Mystical Ark* Bk. IV, XV): you, small, are melted into wanting, imagination here and before subverting the effervescence of imagination.

.   .   .

Richard of St. Victor's fifth and sixth stages of contemplation, consider craning intelligence that is above but not beyond reason and above and against reason. The mystical theology he describes in *The Mystical Ark* comes from an allegorical reading of the construction of the ark of the covenant (Exod. 25:10 ff): in the highest forms of contemplation, his text is the two golden cherubim that Moses is instructed to place on either side of the throne of mercy, their stretched wings overshadowing it. "Cherub" represents fullness of knowledge; the figures are angelic, symbolizing an intelligence within human range, yet beyond the power of human reason (*The Mystical Ark* Bk. IV, I), being beyond sense experience and, in the case of the second cherub, beyond similtude: they are made of hammered gold—one comes to this knowing through compunction rather than investigation, through sighs, through lamentation (*The Mystical Ark* Bk. IV, VI). It is ecstatic knowledge, entry into "the lofty secret places of divine incomprehensibility." The right-hand cherub represents knowledge that reason cannot discover yet can confirm, announcing some commensurability between human and divine things, a scale, "divine similitude in rational substances"; the left-hand cherub "stands on the side of dissimilitude" (*The Mystical Ark* Bk. IV, VIII): both sorts of knowledge are available only through showing or the witness of authority: one is either swept here or led.

Each of the cherubim's wings is outstretched: their "continual stretching" is the eagerness of the ecstatic mind for divine contemplation "in every place, at every time," the pursuit of it everywhere with longing, waiting for the divine showing without relief, in unbroken suspense, alert, compuncted. Waiting — Elijah's waiting at the entrance of the cave, face covered, is emblematic (1 Kings 19:13; *The Mystical Ark* Bk. IV, X) — replaces here the probe of reason.

·   ·   ·

Desire is strange; it breeds estrangement; desire is strange: it seems distant; delivered yet not assumable; larger-than-self; the self quintessentially. Desire appears to stand outside, ingenious, telos-scenting, gusting. It enacts a work in whom God chooses: it refuses the causality of merit (45); it infiltrates the contemplative and becomes the vector and the haste of his interiority: desire follows the delight of God, is what one cannot know likes (45), is the joy of this external force. Intimate, kidnapping, lifting, disconcerting, beneficent, its push and easy pull make it nothing other than desire, yet it is not this "but a thing thou knowest never what, that stirrest thee to will and desire thou knowest never what" (45–6), a meta-personal exigence, unreadable, seemingly supplanting the self.

It cannot be chosen, cannot be manufactured; what one most elementally needs — union with the source of being, the larger self of oneness — is not even desirable without this work begun within one, not even desirable unless one has the single desire that alone can desire it: the soul without this sent impulse is not alive (45). This stirring makes you *atopos* — the nonerotic mutter — it makes you unlike yourself, stripping you of the use of sight, reason, affect, imagination, thrusting you toward the upset and nonrefusability of the cloud.

. . .

Desire may be built and shaped by hesychastic exclamations (SIN, GOD); in time, it nudges into sorrow: a raw sense of self appears to stand between the contemplative and the pulling cloud, a "lump of sin," the individual apprehended as essentially malaligned by cupidity. This sense arises with sorrow; only "ghostly sorrow" can relieve it, this "naked knowing and feeling" of one's being (56). This corrective sorrow is penthos, the experience of tears in Cassian through which the soul comes to be inflamed, is brought to the mute "prayer of fire" (*Conf.* 9: 25–7). This sadness that is prayer, is erotic, is not despair: if it truly comes from desire, it leans toward discretion (54) even in the matter of tears; it eschews all sorts of strain. Penthos smooths the impulse to self: in it, the self is felt as a congealed mass of inaptness. Felt thus it occludes less the passage to the cloud, while strained simulacra of this work, melodramatic dolour, rococo physical effects, are vanities, the self gaudily asserted, blocking the encounter with divine opacity.

One enters the counterfeits of ghostly sorrow through literalism — a "fleshly and bodily" apprehension of compunction in which the novice labours to produce a sensation of interior burning (58), compunction as physical symptom — and the refusal of counsel. If one is not impelled by desire in this work, he is incapable of a lyrical reading of this possible sorrow; the pliancy of waiting is beyond him. He has no ear for such response: he plunges ahead with a perilous muscularity (59). The desire that breeds sorrow, that breeds flame, avoids the inattention of presumption; self-effaced, alert for the unanticipatable, unmingled with externality, ghostly, it will hide itself and grow (60). The substance of all perfection is a good will — Augustine's *Tota vita christiani boni sanctum desiderium est*: a good will is acquiescence to the desire — appearing as sorrow, appearing as loneliness, appearing as reach — visited on the contemplative (63); if one is truly erotic, he will believe, further, that desire has nothing to do with consolation (64), and will seek neither the consolation nor the desire.

. . .

Desire chastens language: it halts what is meant ghostly from being appropriated bodily. Without the "work of this book," however, the visitation of this keen, nondirectable stirring, one's understanding will be inevitably anti-metaphorical, and one will be led into various grotesqueries of interiority as a result. This is especially true with the words "in" and "up"; read literally, they produce pitched affectation—"some set their eyes in their head as though they were sturdy sheep beaten in the head, and as though they should die anon. Some hang their heads on one side, as if a worm were in their ears. Some pipe when they should speak..." (67). Read a psychagogic book such as *The Cloud* as something other than suggestive, pointing, as phenomenological encouragement to those already caught in the work, and it will produce strain and posturing: it could drive the nonerotic mad (66).

To hear resonantly, playfully, compellingly, heuristically, yieldingly—as one would receive metaphor—what is meant psychagogically is a sign one is exercised by desire's work. The nonerotic cannot stop themselves from reading psychagogic remarks as physical description, as analysis, as physical injunction, this misreading a sign of their unengaged state; it is a quick step from this to unseemly behaviour that is presumptuous, exhibitionistic, driven by a plain greed for hidden things. A literal construal is disastrous because it is too accommodating to human categories (73): it is aggrandizement, not fecund loss. The nonerotic are anti-metaphorical; literalism proofs them against the upheaval in an encounter with the cloud, so nothing new comes from their efforts beyond more outlandish enshrinements of the status quo. They are not moved; they do not move.

. . .

Someone who takes up this work, is lifted by this dynamism, is governed by it and is brought to beauty, says *The Cloud* (69), oddly both physical and interior beauty, so that he will come to seem attractive, no matter how ill-favoured in appearance he may have been. Such beauty comes from a particular sort of seeing, one where the vigorously anthropomorphic imagination, the sentimental imagination, have scant place: the effort to pierce the heavens with one's eyes, the belief that one has such special powers of beholding, are leagued with both fanatical conviction and massive efforts of self-promotion.

> These men will sometimes with the curiosity of their imagination pierce the planets, and make a hole in the firmament to look in thereat. These men will make a God as they like and clothe him full richly in clothes, and set him on a throne, far more curiously than ever was he depicted on this earth. These men will make angels in bodily likeness, and set them about, each one with diverse minstrelsy, far more curious than ever was any seen or heard in this life (73).

When the impulse to religious clarity, the impulse to arrive at complete ontological accounts, are seen as apogeal cognitive states, one tilts to polyform ugliness, is a threat both to oneself and others, though the danger is apparent only to the erotic. When one's thinking has lost the indeterminacy, waiting, ambivalence, proteanness of metaphor and heuristic, it has lost all erotic qualities and shunts toward the burlesque, the self-inflated, the judgemental and dogmatic.

The project to map interior states, the cognitive ambition to make all visualizable, is the sign of an unmusical being; this ambition sinks the one who has it further into unmusicality. To misread, say, "lift up," "go in," "stirring," and "rest" as physical directions, this tin ear toward the nature of psychagogic utterance, is to depart from the practice in which one supposes one is engaged: it is not only wrong reading, but also is antagonistic to beauty. All bodily things must be sublated to ghostly things (78); even what is fully rendered, such as Christological doctrine, must be read, as well, as heuristic—that is, understood in desire (78)—to be complete. A lyrical sensibility in ghostly matters alone alters the soul to beauty: here is the height of cognition for it can transform. Be nowhere, then, *The Cloud* advises, not in, up, beyond: starve the mind of images on which to work.

> And although thy bodily wits can find there nothing to feed them on, for they think it nought that thou dost, yea: do on then this nought, and do it for God's love. And cease not, therefore, but travail busily in that nought with a watchful desire to will to have God, whom no man may know. For I tell thee truly that I had rather be so nowhere bodily, wrestling with that blind nought, than be so great a lord that I might, when I would, be everywhere bodily, merrily playing with all this aught as a lord with his own (86).

Labour "fast" in this nought, the book urges; the labour is a hurtling noetic darkness; all that remains is attention that is unconsoled, imageless, homeless, pressing, craning toward the beautiful daimonic thing that draws from the other side of names, representation, analysis, sight, yet which may be touched in desire. Successive readings of such books as *The Cloud of Unknowing* will accomplish this stripping of desire's reach and assist in its acceleration.

III

Six
....

GOING HOME

W HEN I moved on to that forty acres that so changed me, minimalist hills I later discovered were sandhills, called on old maps the Moosewood Sandhills, delta of an ancient river, what I eventually came to like about the place was its boniness. Even before I planted a garden, before I started cutting poplar deadfall, blow-down, for the stove we put in after two years, when I was just moving around on it, starting to be able to pick out deer trails, I liked the way the land gave almost nothing. It was so blond, friable, dry, intractable, threadbare. But at the very beginning, the first six months, the first winter, all of this worried me — a little grass, blow-outs where there was bare sand below an overhanging thatch of jumper roots — there wasn't enough for the eye: I thought I'd starve. I remembered one of the apothegmata Merton had collected: if you don't manage to take in the genius of the place, let it say its piece through you, the place will throw you out. And I saw that these hills, these poplar islands, could just shrug me off, no problem. With some desperation, I drove myself to find a way into the good graces of this particular bit of land. I didn't have any other place else to go; I couldn't manage being sent away. But I had no confidence I could learn to bed down where events had brought me.

. . .

I hadn't lived in Saskatchewan for almost fifteen years, though I'd been back for visits. Being here now was different: no plane back, no somewhere else. Things presented themselves differently. And I discovered that it was almost impossible for me to breathe here: everything, I realized, looking around, still in the city, that had shaped my growing up in Regina, churches, the university, sports teams, buildings downtown—the triumphalism of a prairie town—all appeared to coast a foot or so off the ground; and this floating made me feel strangely breathless. Or sometimes it seemed as if all of it was leaning backward from this place as if it were caught in a gust of longing for some old country, some metropolis, wherever the action currently was believed to be. What had been built here didn't seem to move easily in the body of the locale; this whole massive effort of civilization put together through incredible effort by European settlers and their descendants appeared tentative, seemed to have its eye on some other place, waiting for judgement; it was elsewhere. It appeared ready to move at any moment. I realized that at forty, though I had been probed by many psychologists, spent eight years in Jesuit formation, read many books, I had done nothing to educate myself to be someone who could live with facility, familiarity, where he was born. This incompetence, when I finally saw it, floored me. Then we moved on to the land, and I saw I really was in trouble.

. . .

We need to find our own way to take this place into our mouth; we must re-say our past in such a way that it will gather us here.

. . .

This place is so unlike us — all places, maybe, but this place especially — many, as a result, of our gestures toward it have been graceless: the busy program to plant forests on the plains started at Dundurn and other military bases, so that the land could look like landscape and we could love it, the relentless use, these days, of chem-fallow. Finally we just filled it with our will, so that the land came to look tired in its heart: almost empty but crammed with human intention, sick with a sameness that came from us.

. . .

Between 1990 and 1999, I patrolled two pieces of terrain, the Moosewood Sandhills and the South Saskatchewan River between Pike Lake and Fish Creek, the hills and river section in north-central Saskatchewan just where short-grass prairie enters aspen parkland. And I tried to make sense of what I was doing in this endless pacing and looking, lying down and looking. I felt pulled, of course; I felt I bad been assigned a post; but I could make very little sense of what I was up to. I worried a single thought for nearly ten years: how to be here? I thought that the European intellectual tradition, our form of interiority, had very little to offer someone transfixed by a question like this—Christianity preoccupied by dogmatic clarification, Greek philosophy construed as ur-rationalism, experimental science—ontologies that traditionally had appeared to obliterate the beckoning weirdness of specificity. None offered a quiet path into things, in none, it seemed, the abashed decorum that appeared appropriate in approaching the distant, unlike world. Only eros, a probe originating in me, that knew nothing, was empty, pressing, seemed promising—longing, loneliness for things, a nostalgia for a hyperbolic state of union that likely originated in nothing other than an attempt by desire itself to describe its own unchecked imagination. So I wrote and thought and talked, and seemed to move not at all on my question. I read the underside of the old tradition, the whispered part, the *Phaedrus,* the *Symposium,* the *Republic,* various collections of desert apothegmata, Cassian's *Conferences, The Mystical Theology, The Divine Names, Periphyseon, The Cloud of Unknowing, Gravity and Grace,* read them in a full-tilt heterodox way, read them as the erotic masterpieces of the West: and I tried to watch what my own desire did. The three books I wrote over this period, *Moosewood Sandhills, Living in the World As If It Were Home, To the River,* were an attempt to track some sort of erotic unfolding going on at the same time in me. I believe that the contemplative focus described with such phenomenological rigour in the texts from antiquity and the Middle Ages could be turned to a place, to a profusion of familiar objects in a locale, without any change in its form or diminishment of its vitality. I am still thinking the same thought, but in another quadrant now, still walking, still homeless where I am. Desire shows more of itself, its unanticipatable meandering.

The more I turned things over in my mind, the more the conviction grew that attention to eros seemed more promising than commitment to any ontology or to any ethics. Consanguinity or the impulse to this seemed more fecund than analytic knowing, the thing for which I had been educated to reach — and this erotic proximity, it finally dawned on me, came only through the stripping of wanting.

·   ·   ·

What does desire do as it unfolds? Is there necessity here? A riverbed? I read Plato — the feather master — tried to read him by burrowing beneath the usual interpretations, then carefully pored over the book he read for erotic instruction: the *Odyssey.* The long, watery striving in that poem, the mammoth, unparalleled affliction of the mind-bright man, the man of many turns, who knows every trick, sleepy, inventive, shimmering Odysseus, resourceful, immaculately solitary, the one who always remembers home, the untrustworthy one, the graced, rash man who becomes nothing other than his longing for home, the sleepy one, his yearning materializing into a journey along the axis mundi itself—here was the paradigm for the range of what Plato wanted to say about desire, here the example that unbridled his speech. Late capitalism's nomadism, its own particular pursuit of home-lessness, its sad, weary anarchy—no wonder few of us now are erotic: who could endure the full range of her yearning in this always-blunting milieu, who could inch toward it, pull off this feat of inching toward it? Everything drifts toward money's unintended telos of placelessness; we are not craning, not small, hurt by rootlessness; we are disas-trously kept, "healed" of a saving disquiet—so how can we be where we are?

· · ·

Corral, Frenchman River valley, southwestern Saskatchewan, early spring, 1999, still snow in the berry thickets along the coulee sides, a big wind out of the northwest. The fence doesn't hold anything now: it's like a failed argument for the immortality of the soul: everything dies. More than a fence, it tingles with numberless pressings toward a precise suffi-ciency; old, it is a museum of muscled anxiety that, to calm itself, has tried to flicker into the near-invisibility of utility. The medieval strain of it—the fence, like abstract argument, has the fly-like suppleness of pure design; it needs no real weight: the force of intention, the mass of ingenuity, fix it to the earth. Like argument, too, it brings the thin consolation within the belief in the therapeutic nature of intricacy: structural complexity matches the world a map, a discipline.

Something has been thrown massively into the fence: it is oiled with masculinity; there can be nothing of the one who made it that remained in reserve; he has crammed himself into what is made; the distance of the maker—the cool remove, the utilitarian calculation—doesn't show in his work. He isn't aloof from his tool; he's "gone bush" in this empty place, but what he's bolted into is not the strangeness of things here, but the false balm of *technē*. There is a pacing inside the tool.

The five strands of barbed wire are attached to large posts, which look implausibly like split-rail cedar (there is no cedar for miles and miles) and which are still rooted deeply, by lengths of still more barbed wire, one piece twisted around itself twenty times or more. Picture the hunkered, black weight of the shoulders and forearms behind this wrenching. But why use barbed wire in the first place as tie wire? Instead of clipping off his excess wire, he's drawn it back into the fence, looping it around each of his five strands, a dawdle and a decoration, a speaking of wire.

One corner post has been secured by punching long lengths of barbed wire under a heavy piece of pink granite; he's somehow dug under the stone to do this. The other three corner posts are attached to two-inch-thick steel rods driven deep: the maul has curled the dark metal at the end of each.

Between the cedar posts, every six inches, he's wired in diamond willow branches he's collected from clumps along the stumpy, brown Missouri-seeking river. There are at least four hundred of these twisted into the wire.

The fence, beautiful, mildly monstrous, is a mimesis of what? I cannot think the man who made it did not also make a little money. A lushness in the wire points that way. Another corral, same style, is on an alkali flat a little farther west in the valley, it, too, unused in sixty years.

Say he throws the pliers in the wagon and moves off. What sort of meal does he return to? I see a single supper, bachelor's delight, out of cans, supplemented by some quick frying. I also can imagine a meal produced intently, right on time, by a woman with red hands, lots of meat, potatoes, bread, coffee, pie. Either way, a thick, male solitude.

. . .

Some tasks appear endless, many-personed—the building of the Panama Canal, the space program. Some of these long tasks are now mostly interior: the Great Depression; the First World War; the Second World War; the Holocaust; the Aboriginal loss of land, culture, a way of life: these must be worked on through a number of lifetimes, turned over and over; with some of them the chill will never leave the bones. Descendants of European settlers are so recently embarked on the undertaking of learning to be in western North America we hardly know we're engaged in it. Being autochthonic, learning to be spoken by the grass and cupped hills. And what we must learn is not geography, not an environmental ethics, not a land-benign economics, not a history, not respect, but a style that is so much ear, so attentive, it cannot step away from its listening and give a report of itself. It thus can't be taught—to attempt this would be to present a bogus norm capable only of fashioning dogmatism, some unearned conviction: but it can be participated in.

. . .

Desire, at its furthest stretch, intimate and outlandish, seems to have the lack of regularity, the ferality, of a strange mountain range: yield to its drift, its articulation, and it will position you in unguessable ways. Inventive, amassing, it is still easily blocked, even more easily tipped into forms that seem to resemble it but that are in fact ways of leaving it under the camouflage of apparent erotic engagement. Dogmatic conviction, wholehearted charm, keen immersion in the status quo, any form of hypertrophied certitude, philosophy of the usual sort: forms of exile from eros, "passion," ways to step from eros's momentum, to dodge its emptying, yet not feel the bite of self-betrayal.

. . .

Mary Oliver says the house you build is a dream-shape come to life. I built a root cellar in the late summer of 1991 when I was at my most confused with the land; I began the whole thing on little more than a whim late one afternoon when I started to dig into the south face of a low hill behind the house; I kept digging for three weeks, into the time of the earliest frosts, until I could no longer throw the dirt high enough to make it over my growing mounds. I made it down eight feet, nine feet—at around six feet I found curiously shaped stones and a curve of deer bones. I poured footings for a seven-by-seven-foot room, set in lag bolts, inserted a bottom plate over them, and built the walls. I had to stop often to drive into town to get books from the library to tell me what to do. I put the heaviest possible insulation into the walls and laid down a flat roof that I covered with straw bales, and then I buried the whole structure, later digging a ramp through the packed wet sand to the door. I knew the scrub land would eventually grow over the building but I got the process moving by throwing crested wheat seed on the mound; I left an opening in the roof for a length of black pipe to stick out, an air hole. I used to sleep in the buried house on hot nights through the following summer; I was looking for dreams: it was a place to wait. The root cellar was chunky, thick-faced, dumb, stone-handed, intent: I thought I'd brought into the world a homunculus, thought I'd extruded a covert part of myself. I later saw it, after I'd done all the work, as some sort of listening post a distance out in the unknown terrain, the land that baffled me and the other world beside that world. God knows what I was after. I haven't seen the root cellar in years; I sometimes imagine that it's disappeared entirely, backed into the hill, fused.

. . .

Both ontologies and goodness have ossifying effects. Ontology points you toward intelligibilities, "presences," your imagination places in the world; the practice this generates is that of the self-addressing one of the many hand puppets the imagination wears. Goodness tips naturally into rectitude, its moral narcissism; perhaps all along it was simply rectitude's finest name. So both systematizing pursuits—the one reaching for an understanding of essence, the other for an ethics—produce solipsistic practices, ways of standing apart from the world. But negative theology—where ravished desire goes when pointed toward something it can never say but can't turn from—isn't know-nothing-ism, nor is it laissez-faire desiring: erotic reach is effective only if it is toward something that arrests you, impoverishes, pulls, something that names you yet seems inarticulably strange: eros pulls you home only if it is in the gravitational field of something unassimilably beautiful. One mustn't conflate injunctions concerning practice with assertions about the nature of the world; if you bow toward the world, it doesn't mean you must imagine shards of divinity inserted in it as a hidden, higher reality; in fact, to so imagine is to turn yourself away from the world as the world entirely. It is to leave it.

. . .

My grandfather lost his wife, Florence Densley Blaylock, in the spring of 1929, then, shortly after, the two small farms he worked in the area around Sequin School, not far from Gooseberry Lake, northeast of Creelman, Saskatchewan. He moved from farm to rented farm in the early 1930s, his four daughters leaving home at thirteen or fourteen to work for local families. During the harvest of 1940, he began to work for a big farmer in the Kipling area named Gus Link; this man was good to him, and he stayed there a few years, but he would not stay forever. For the rest of his life he moved around as a farm labourer: in his fifties, during the last years of the war, he was working on a ranch near Kelowna. My uncle Jack, his youngest child, told his father he was going into town sometime in the late summer of 1940, took the train into Regina instead, got drunk on cheap wine, and passed out under the leaves of bolting, frost-touched rhubarb in the garden behind my mother's rooming house. He joined the army the next day, lying about his age, and later broke a leg in training in England the day before his regiment took part in the Dieppe raid. Later still he fought in France and Holland. Very little else was said about this or any other family event; the stories my mother and aunts tell have an atomic sort of economy: this happened, then this, nothing more. I used to see this as reticence, but now it appears to me to be as a sort of mild, oblique *amor fati*.

. . .

Desire can bring you to a good place, approaching paradisiac unions, if it is pulled by quintessential occurrence, fabulous, unlikely, provoking the whole of wanting, something whose power to draw will lead you to believe you remember it from before: correcting desire appears unexpectedly as nostalgia. Being utterly disarmed by something beautiful, a moral gesture, a person, can be such an occurrence: again you will seem to remember. You will *see* a surpassing thing and know you have seen it as it is; you will realize you have always known it was without parallel even if it had not always been present in memory.

. . .

My aunt had a lung removed shortly before Christmas this past winter; she wasn't that far from her eighty-fifth birthday, so, maybe not surprisingly, she never recovered from the procedure, though she lived a further two months. She wasn't in pain—this, apparently, was the point of the surgery—but her death shocked her when it came into view. I happened to be in Edmonton that year, at the university, and was one of the few of her family in the city; I took her to see the doctor about the "spot" they'd recently discovered on her lung. I believe she thought she'd dodge this bullet, that she'd be told, after waiting more than two hours with others facing hard news, that the thing actually was an old tubercular scar. She was staggered, of course, once she learned her true state, but even as we pulled from the winter parking lot, it was obvious she was settling into herself to lift a cloudy weight.

. . .

We must start again learning how to be in this place, or at least I must. We begin from scraps. We should learn the names for things as a minimum — not to fulfill taxonomies but as acts of courtesy, for musical reasons, entering the gesture of decorum. Part of such naming will be being quiet, useless, broken maybe, if one is lucky: perhaps something will come toward us. Read the shit, read the deer trails. Practise an activism of forgetting the royalty of one's name, of yielding, of stepping aside. This will be like breathing through the whole body, the new, larger body of a place that might take us in.

The world, though, will stay nameless, even as we learn our names for it, and this, though it may appear to be, is not erotic failure. A sense of the distance of things has a wonderful ascetic effect: it breeds deference; it provides optimum growing conditions for admiration. Then we may be fed and taught; knowing, in the end, is being looked after. It, this farness, returns us to our sober selves by relieving us of our self-ministrations, our self-priesting assurances that all is well or somehow will be. I'll keep to this distance, I say to myself — without any loss of desire for the far things.

Seven

GETTING INTO THE CABRI LAKE AREA

Go to Leader, Saskatchewan, and stay at the hotel across from the elevators if it's too cold to sleep on the river flat just north of the Estuary townsite. Estuary is west and north of Leader—you'll have to pass by it eventually: only five houses or so left, two last summer with trucks parked in the yard, another one, a white bungalow, set off to the west nearer the river, owned, rumour has it, by an American hunter who turns up every fall or so. Anyway, the Leader hotel. It's old, smells of cigarette smoke climbing through the ceiling from the small bar below; you could read the paper through the sheets. On the weekends, they have a buffet in the evening and morning. The town is doing well; a number of people there work at the Petro-Canada plant at Burstall, a forty-five-minute drive southwest. If you arrive on a Friday night, visit the Swiss owner of the men's store the next morning before you set out: lots of stories and some interesting merchandise aimed at Hutterite colonies in the area.

Come down into the river valley past the old Estuary cemetery and the abandoned town: the large cement rectangle rising out of the grass with the square hole is the old safe of the Standard Bank. To the west is Bull's Head, an oddly shaped, high bluff facing the confluence of the Red Deer and the South Saskatchewan Rivers, deep water at the base of it, good for fishing. I've heard talk that this is where Big Bear had his vision in the 1800s. The ferry runs irregularly; if the man is on the other side when you get there, he'll see you and come over. Turn right when you've risen out of the valley and the valley's elm thicket and follow that crooked road east into the sun—just as it bends north you might see some clouds of white dust heaving up in the distance, winds coming off a large alkaline plain. That's where you're headed, Cabri Lake. You'll have to walk from the road, a long walk, cropped land, pasture, marsh, then a stretch no one seems to be doing anything with—I saw a huge coyote there last year: its head at first made me think it was a sheep. If you do manage to get into the land around the lake and talk to anyone about this, keep your directions to the place as vague as these.

. . .

The ascesis of staying where you are: your cell will teach you everything. I don't know anything right now. The land is there and I am here and I don't know anything. I keep lifting my mind to the light and peering in: nothing. My sort of people have always been moving through — Alberta looks good these days, they say, maybe British Columbia — tuned to the anarchic flux of capitalism, a little too bright, a touch off plumb, with alacrity.

. . .

The acme of speech is language that carries the knowledge of its inevitable failure inside it: the word cannot be circumscription; it cannot name; it can't even confess with accuracy. But it still loves — helplessly — the world and so walks alongside it; it says what it loves is a red, red rose, says it's a sunset, dusk over a river, and names nothing with this, misspeaks what it points to but hears and reports a moan deep within the speaker. Such language can't identify what it wishes to name, but it somehow manages to achieve a greater interior proximity to that thing. This is desire's speech, of course: beauty makes you lonely; beauty gives you a sweat of plans; thick, multilayered beauty makes you homeless. You must have close to nothing for any of this to happen, though, it seems. Lyric language is a companion along this way — it doesn't know what it's saying. The highest theology, pseudo-Dionysius says, is not definitional but hymnal: praise and wait for something to take you in.

. . .

Another interesting place to go is the sandhills around Senlac, half a day north — sleep in the truck at the regional park there, close to the Alberta border, or take a room at the Sunset Motel, fifteen dollars a night the last time I was a guest. There's a large Manitou Lake at the north end of the huge range of treed-in dunes a little south of Neilburg, strange mounds surrounding it; there are abandoned towns scattered throughout the area, Artland, Winter, lots of community pasture and dirt roads, a place that could rub away a large part of your name. Most of the pasture is contiguous; once the cows are off, you could walk, you sense, forever.

. . .

Language that doesn't know what it's doing; desire that doesn't know where it's headed: I spend most of my time listening and hear pretty well nothing. Maybe I've run out of gas; maybe (against all odds) I'm being obedient to the last real thing I've heard. A nice place to go for breakfast is the Senlac Café. In the beer parlour at night: oil workers and long-time drinking buddies, some just returning from a brief retirement from the booze. The Anglican church in town is definitely unused; it looks as if they might open up the United church for funerals. All of the names of the streets have a British ring: Hastings, William. The cenotaph at the centre of town has a plaque for the Great War with eleven names on it.

. . .

This is what I can tell you about Cabri Lake: a large salt flat surrounded by high brown hills. My guess, based on the size of the alkaline clouds the wind was lifting, is that it would take a day to walk from the south to the north end—likely you wouldn't find any water as you went along: grass, grass, grass, then the big salt pan. I didn't get any farther than the hills to the south of the white flat; that's where I saw the coyote ambling along, tilting its nose now and then until its nostrils were parallel with the wind; it didn't see us, didn't even appear to be wary—who comes into these parts anyway?

You will find water, though, as you approach the southern hills, a couple of ponds, a stream, and a salt marsh; take the east hillside of the stream as you move north: the west shore just leads you deeper into the marsh and that sort of mud can be unforgiving. I saw a godwit in one of the ponds you pass as you come toward the marsh.

There is a story that there is a large human effigy in the grass flats around the empty lake, or possibly in the surrounding hills, well hung, ecstatic; someone saw it from a small plane thirty years or so ago, and there was a newspaper report I vaguely remember. Your chances of finding it on foot are about nil. Or maybe it was seen farther east in the Great Sandhills; I haven't heard any mention of it in a long time.

. . .

The Western contemplative tradition, Plato to Weil, and from even before Plato, his Odyssean, shamanic precursors, is a simple story: desire and having nothing; being scraped down until you can see beauty; beauty itself scraping you down. The idea is to get to positionless responsivity: utter permeability guarded by the temple dogs of collection and division: this, say the dogs, is genuine advance, that is plain cleverness. This pair comes toward you out of anamnesis, an experience of beauty so strong it makes you half crazy and gives you the strange sense that you remember now some early, perfect time when you simply knew. Such an experience both ruins you—you will be ever unlike—and is the way home. They will come up to you, the two dogs of discernment, friendly but not domesticated, animals out of the forest, and snuffle your hand. This in itself will be disconcerting.

Be as available to the right sort of daimonic exigence, says John Cassian, as a bit of down is to wind: the pure state is erotic nomadism: take this position as, at least, heuristic, and let it work you down.

. . .

Two other good places to get into are the valley of the Frenchman River, east and south of the Cypress Hills, and Rock Creek valley, in the East Block of Grasslands National Park, both part of the northern limit of the Missouri drainage. Go in winter if you can; you will be able to walk the river: the ice is thick enough except where beaver chew pokes out and has made a small rapids; there you'll find open water even in the coldest weather. Listen to the river and you will be able to make out these places, current gurgle, current splash against ice, or simply follow the trail animals have made, mule deer, coyote, fox: cougar, people say, are moving east along all the river valleys, tracking an explosion in the white tail population.

A friend, Don McKay, and I came in here three or so winters ago, mid-February, and spent one day slogging through waist-deep drifts down the coulees along the valley sides, having left our snowshoes in the truck: the valley top had no more than half a foot of snow on it and we thought we could safely forget the shoes. The next day we walked east along the river, coyotes sounding in sequence along one side of the valley, across the flats and up and along the other side in the afternoon. We found the odd kill site, but not too much else appeared to be happening in the wide, white place. When you come, you can stay either at the rancher's bar in Val Marie or the re-fitted convent on the southern edge of town.

The bar in Mankota is a good place to eat if you are coming in late from the east.

It would be difficult to get into the East Block in winter: there's only a track from the gravel road and, of course, it's not ploughed; few people go there, so no trail would be broken. You might make it if the snow cover is very light; close all gates after you pass through: someone is wintering cattle here and would appreciate your courtesy.

But if you can't get into the East Block in winter, try late summer after the golden eagle brood has fledged on the bluff where Rock Creek bends south. Come in from the north; that's the route everyone takes, but maps show there's an entry on the west, though I've never felt eager to try it. In the winter, that way wouldn't be worth the risk; people don't seem to live out there, and there simply would be no way in; you could get stuck and freeze. A sudden rain in summer would strand you in gumbo. But it might be worth a try in dry weather. Do a little shopping in Rockglen before you come down this way, and plan to spend a few days. The hills around are badlands, clay with rich, grassy drainage clefts; there are antelope through here, some impressive rubbing stones. Camp anywhere.

. . .

Being in a place demands a practice: it isn't tourism or Romanticism: things aren't laid on, nor are they occultly given: here the practice is putting yourself out there and walking. There is almost always a wall of fear to pass through as you undertake an exercise like this, the temptation to turn the truck back at Rockglen or Wood Mountain, to stay not so long, to forget the whole thing. It's nervousness around being *atopos*, I think, being culpably away from others, wasting time: maybe what comes up to you won't be friendly. Push a little on it and the blockage yields somewhat. Do what you can; walk and see where it gets you. The walking, though, is not an instrument, not a means to arrive at some chthonic accord; as you walk, you are already as there as you're going to get, though you hardly feel this: the reeling, toppling condition of always wanting is as close as anyone gets to grace.

The Cabri Lake area—I think I'll go back there this spring, or maybe I'll curve up to Gronlid and Arborfield at the edge of the Pasquia Hills wilderness, thick aspen bush on the border of the northern forest—I've been wanting to stop in at Arborfield for years. I don't know what I'm doing, and when I listen I hear nothing, my ear embedded in a blank on the band. I'll go where this not-speaking, not-hearing urges: it's a thin road, but little else is on offer. Ruby Rosedale community pasture, Montrose community pasture: walking in the fall is best when the light is exhausted, one of the last hawks circling overhead, too high for hunting, and the distance seems to drink you a bit at a time.

NOTES

INTRODUCTION

1 The phrase is Patricia Cox Miller's and appears in her essay "'In My Father's House Are Many Dwelling Places': κτισα in Origen's *De Principiis*," in *Anglican Theological Review* 62, 1980, p. 336.

2 Coleridge claimed the rhythmic regularity of Wordsworth's poetry was an aural replication of the author's habit of pacing on gravelled walkways as he composed; Coleridge himself preferred thrashing through thickets; this preference is clear in the rhythms of his own work. Osip Mandelstam believed Dante's music, particularly in the *Purgatorio,* glorified "the human gait, the measure and rhythm of walking." Osip Mandelstam, "Conversation About Dante," in *Mandelstam, The Complete Critical Prose and Letters,* ed. Jane Gary Harris, trans. Jane Gary Harris and Constance Link (Ann Arbor, Mich.: Ardis, 1979), p. 400.

3   See Zdravko Planinc, *Plato's Political Philosophy* (Columbia, Mo.:
     University of Missouri Press, 1991) and "Homeric Imagery in
     Plato's *Phaedrus*," in *Politics, Philosophy, Writing: Plato's Art of Caring
     for Souls* (Columbia, Mo.: University of Missouri Press, 2001) for
     an illuminating account of Plato's considerable debt to Homer,
     as well as his project to depict Socrates as the "new Odysseus."
     Planinc's work here is crucial to any penetrating understand-
     ing of Plato.

One

PHILOSOPHICAL APOKATASTASIS:
ON WRITING AND RETURN

1   Robert Bringhurst, *A Story as Sharp as a Knife: The Classical Haida
     Myth Tellers and Their World.* (Vancouver: Douglas and McIntyre,
     1999), pp. 76–99. Bringhurst draws parallels between Homeric
     and Haida epic poetry, in particular the poems dictated by
     Skaay and Ghandl to ethnologist John Swanton in the early
     years of the twentieth century in Haida Gwaii, the islands on
     the boundary between the worlds. The poems share psycha-
     gogic patterns as well as literary traits.

2   Zdravko Planinc,"Homeric Imagery in Plato's *Phaedrus*"; E. A. S.
     Butterworth, *Some Traces of the Pre-Olympian World in Greek Literature
     and Myth* (Berlin: De Gruyter, 1966), pp. 98–173; E. R Dodds, *The
     Greeks and the Irrational* (Berkeley: University of California Press,
     1964), pp. 135–78; Charles Olson, *Olson: The Journal of the Charles*

Olson Archives #10 (Storrs, Conn.: University of Connecticut Library, 1978), pp. 78 and 91; Agathe Thornton, *People and Themes in Homer's Odyssey* (London: Metheun, 1970), pp. 16–37.

3 See Mircea Eliade, *Shamanism: Archaic Techniques of Ecstasy*, trans. Willard R. Trask (Princeton: Princeton University Press, Bollingen Series LXXVI, 1992), pp. 76–7.

Two
WHERE DESIRE GOES

1 Simone Weil, "God in Plato," in *On Science. Necessity, and the Love of God* (London: Oxford University Press, 1968), pp. 124ff. Weil describes the "shock" of an encounter with beauty—moral, intellectual, physical, political—as the beginning of a higher spiritual life.

2 See note 3 in the translation of the dialogue by Alexander Nehemas and Paul Woodruff.

Three
HOW CASSIAN READ

1 *Lausiac History*, 55.3.
2 *Praktikos*, 87. "The man who is progressing in the ascetic life diminishes the force of passion. The man progressing in contemplation diminishes ignorance. As regards the passions,

the time will come when they will be entirely destroyed. In the matter of ignorance, however, one type will have an end, but another type will not." This claim recalls Gregory of Nyssa's notion of epektasis. The coincidence of perpetual not-knowing and philosophic eros is as old as Heraclitus.

3   The apothegmatum appears in Thomas Merton, *The Wisdom of the Desert: Sayings of the Desert Fathers of the Fourth Century* (New York: New Directions, 1960), XVII.

4   For another instance of suprarational transfixity, there is Jane Hirshfield, "Secretive Heart," in *The Lives of the Heart* (New York: HarperCollins, 1997), p. 9.

5   Plotinus, *Enneads* 2. 2. 1–2.

6   Martin Luther, *De Servo Arbitria*, WA, 18, 700.

Four
KNOWING AS RITUAL

1   Greek *presbyteros*, elder, comparable with *presbys*, old, an old man; cf. Sanskrit *purugava*, a guide, a leader (originally of a herd of oxen).

2   A full account of the debate occurs in Jaroslav Pelikan's Introduction to *Pseudo-Dionysius, the Complete Works*, Colm Luibheid, trans. (New York: Paulist Press, 1987), pp. 13–15.

3 See Andrew Louth, *The Origins of the Christian Mystical Tradition: From Plato to Denys* (Oxford: Oxford University Press, 1981), p. 161.

4 *Patrologia Latina*, Vol. 122.

5 *The Works of Aristotle*, ed. W. D. Ross (Oxford: Clarendon Press, 1908–31), Vol. 12, fragment 15.

6 Libranius, *Protemplis* 30.8.

7 Gregory Shaw, in *Theurgy and the Soul: the Neoplatonism of Iamblichus* (University Park, Pa.: The Pennsylvania State University Press, 1995), p. 12, argues that Plato's own notion of paideia involved a hierarchical unfolding of the powers of the soul, along with an enfolding of the soul in the harmonies of the cosmos. Much of my discussion on theurgy in this section is indebted to Shaw.

Five

THE WORK OF DESIRE

1 The edition of *The Cloud* used here is edited by Justin McCann O.S.B. (London: Burns and Oates, 1936). There are many renderings of *The Cloud* in modern English, but the McCann version is the most trustworthy.

2 Issac of Stella, Sermon 9, in *Sermons on the Christian Year*, Vol. 1, trans. Hugh McCaffery (Kalamazoo, Mich.: Cistercian Publications, 1979).

FURTHER READING

Armstrong, A. H, ed. *Classical Mediterranean Spirituality: Egyptian, Greek, Roman.* New York: Crossroad, 1986.

Eliade, Mircea. *Shamanism: Archaic Techniques of Ecstasy.* New York: Pantheon, 1992.

Grant, George. *Technology and Empire.* Toronto: House of Anansi Press, 1969.

Hadot, Ilsetraut. "The Spiritual Guide." In *Classical Mediterranean Spirituality, Egyptian, Greek, Roman.* Edited by A. H. Armstrong. New York: Crossroad, 1986.

Hadot, Pierre. *Philosophy as a Way of Life: Spiritual Exercises from Socrates to Foucault.* Translated by Michael Chase. Oxford: Blackwell, 1995.

————. *What Is Ancient Philosophy?* Translated by Michael Chase. Cambridge, Mass.: Harvard University Press, 2002.

Leclerq, Jean. *The Love of Learning and the Desire for God: A Study in Monastic Culture.* Translated by Catharine Misrahi. New York: Fordham University Press, 1961.

Merton, Thomas. *Contemplative Prayer.* New York: Doubleday, 1990.

Planinc, Zdravko. "Homeric Imagery in Plato's Phaedrus." In *Politics, Philosophy, Writing: Plato's Art of Caring for Souls.* Edited by Zdravko Planinc. Columbia, Mo.: University of Missouri Press, 2001.

_____. *Plato's Political Philosophy: Prudence in the "Republic" and the "Laws."* Columbia, Mo.: University of Missouri Press, 1991.

_____. *Plato Through Homer: Poetry and Philosophy in the Cosmological Dialogues.* Columbia, Mo.: University of Missouri Press, 2003.

Rappe, Sara. *Reading Neoplatonism: Non-Discursive Thinking in Plotinus, Proclus, and Damascius.* Cambridge: Cambridge University Press, 2000.

Shaw, Gregory. *Theurgy and the Soul: The Neo-Platonism of Iamblichus.* University Park, Pa: Pennsylvania State University Press, 1995.

Weil, Simone. "God in Plato." In *On Science, Necessity, and the Love of God.* Oxford: Oxford University Press, 1968.

ACKNOWLEDGEMENTS

"Philosophical Apokatastasis: On Writing and Return" and "Going Home" were previously published in *Thinking and Singing: Poetry and the Practice of Philosophy* (Cormorant, 2002). "Getting into the Cabri Lake Area" was printed in *The Eye in the Thicket* (Thistledown Books, 2002, Sean Virgo, editor) and in *Brick* magazine.

The author wishes to thank the Canada Council for the Arts for a Senior Fellowship, which greatly assisted in the writing of this book.

ABOUT THE AUTHOR

TIM LILBURN is a poet and essayist, and the author of eight books of poetry, including *Kill-site, To the River, Moosewood Sandhills,* and most recently *Orphic Politics.* He has been nominated for the Governor General's Award in Literature twice: in 1989, for *Tourist to Ecstasy,* and in 2003, when he received the award for *Kill-site.* He is the author of *Living in the World As If It Were Home,* a book of essays on ecology and desire, and the editor of, and a contributor to, two influential essay collections on poetics, *Poetry and Knowing* and *Thinking and Singing: Poetry and the Practice of Philosophy.* Lilburn's work has been translated into French, Chinese, Serbian, and Polish, and has received the Canadian Authors Association Award, the Saskatchewan Book of the Year Award, and the Saskatchewan Nonfiction Award. Lilburn lives in Victoria, B.C., where he teaches at the University of Victoria.